ISE Appraisal

Application Generators Volume

March 1990

ISE Appraisal and Evaluation
Application Generators Volume

© **Crown Copyright 1990**

First published 1990

ISBN 0 11 330532 X

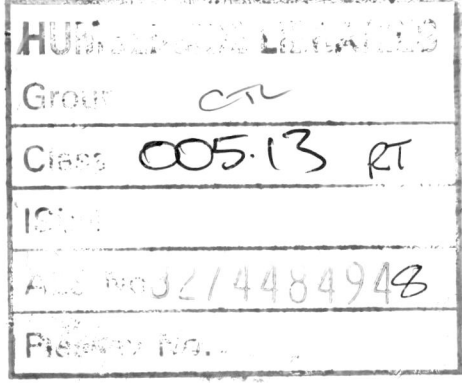

For further information regarding this document please contact :-

Information Systems Engineering Division
CCTA, Norwich
0603 694762

Foreword

This document is the Application Generators volume of the CCTA Information Systems Engineering Appraisal and Evaluation Library. This Library is intended to aid appraisal and evaluation of data management products and consists of an Overview and Procedures volume, together with supporting technology specific volumes.

The Overview and Procedures volume describes the series and provides a procedure for using the criteria contained in the technology specific volumes in a number of contexts. These include making a strategic selection, evaluation during a feasibility study, and evaluation during the procurement stage of a project. The evaluation procedure is placed into the context of other CCTA procedures, such as those for procurement and evaluation, and methods such as SSADM. It has been written in support of the CCTA Information Systems Guides.

Each technology specific volume provides a hierarchy of criteria that may be used as the basis for the evaluation of products in that technology class. The initial volumes will be for Database Management Systems, Knowledge Based Systems, and Application Software Packages; as well as this volume for Application Generators.

This Appraisal and Evaluation Library has been produced to assist organisations to identify the product, or set of products, which best meets their requirements. The procedure and the criteria have developed as technology has changed, and as a result of experience gained from their use. CCTA welcomes comment on, and contributions to, this Library to ensure that it continues to provide maximum benefit.

Contents

Introduction			page
i		General	9
ii		Scope	13
iii		Criteria	19

Chapter			
1		**Generality**	23
	1.1	On-line systems	23
	1.2	Batch systems	27
2		**Usability**	31
	2.1	Specification language	31
	2.2	Application development tools	32
	2.3	Application testing	35
	2.4	Development environment	37
	2.5	Data and application definition	41
3		**Functionality**	43
	3.1	Specification storage	43
	3.2	Specification language	43
4		**Integration with other products**	47
	4.1	Integration with data dictionary	47
	4.2	Integration with DBMS	48
	4.3	Integration with transaction processing system	52
	4.4	Integration with operating system	53
5		**Capabilities of other system components**	57
	5.1	Capabilities of data dictionary	57
	5.2	Capabilities of DBMS	58
	5.3	Capabilities of the TP monitor	58
	5.4	Capabilities of report writer	59
	5.5	Capabilities of query facility	60
6		**Efficiency**	63
	6.1	Development productivity	63
	6.2	Development resource usage	64
	6.3	Runtime resource usage	64

7		**Structured Systems Analysis and Design Methodology**	67
	7.1	Compatibility	67
	7.2	Tool support of SSADM	70
8		**Quality and control**	73
	8.1	Documentation	73
	8.2	Development control	73
	8.3	Audit control	74
	8.4	Quality assurance monitoring	74
	8.5	Performance monitoring and control	75
	8.6	Effect on the organisation	76
9		**Environment independence**	77
	9.1	Hardware independence	77
	9.2	Software independence	77
10		**End user interface**	79
	10.1	Invocation	79
	10.2	Navigation	80
	10.3	Dialogue	80
	10.4	Presentation and rendition	81
	10.5	Variants	82
	10.6	End user help system	82
	10.7	Session concurrency	83
	10.8	Error messages	83
	10.9	Skill levels	83
11		**Security**	85
	11.1	Access control	85
	11.2	Encryption	85
12		**Product Credibility**	87
	12.1	Quality of Product	87
	12.2	Product Development Status	87
	12.3	Supplier Assessment	88
	12.4	Product background	90
	12.5	Documentation	93
	12.6	Training	94
	12.7	Support	94
	12.8	Enhancements	97
	12.9	Related products	97
13		**Project specific requirements**	99

14	**Costs**		101
	14.1	Software	101
	14.2	Hardware	102
	14.3	System operation and maintenance	103
	14.4	People	103
	14.5	Documentation	104
Annex	**Criteria hierarchy**		105

i General

i.1 Background

This document is the technology specific volume on Application Generators of the CCTA Appraisal and Evaluation Library on the subject of application development product appraisal and evaluation.

The objective of this Library is to define a framework for

> 'impartial and effective evaluation to find the product, or products, which best meet the needs and constraints of the organisation'.

The CCTA Information Systems Engineering Division first produced a guide to the Appraisal and Evaluation of Application Generator and Database Management System (DBMS) products in 1986. This document was updated in 1988 and in the process was divided into two volumes, one for Application Generators and one for Database Management Systems.

Several other subject areas have been identified where evaluation criteria may usefully be provided. To avoid duplication of content the common, procedural element, has been separated out into a separate Overview and Procedures volume as part of the Library.

This volume provides technology specific evaluation criteria appropriate to Application Generator products. It should be used with the Overview and Procedures volume.

i.2 The importance of Application Generators

This volume is intended to help in the appraisal and evaluation of AG software. The pace of software development in the late 1980s has helped to create a systems environment for the success of AG products. Because this development has taken place in a highly competitive software marketplace, with open procurement policies, means that implementors, as customers, have opportunities for wide choice.

Data management products are becoming increasingly important; in particular because of their ability to produce high quality, easily maintainable computer systems, faster, and with reduced reliance upon highly skilled technical staff. It does not follow however that the need for thorough systems analysis and design can be dispensed with. Application Generators (AG) are used to develop the applications, and Database Management System (DBMS) are used to implement and maintain the data content.

AG and DBMS products can be obtained from many suppliers, and products from different suppliers can be used together. Therefore separate Application Generator and Database Management Systems volumes have been produced to allow the separate, independent, evaluation of both types of products. The separate assessment of the DBMS and AG components of the software environment reflect the movement of many vendors towards providing 'open systems', in which different components of the environment can be produced by different software vendors. Other software components such as end user Query Facilities and Report Writers probably will also exist within the environment but are likely to be of lesser importance.

i.3 Audience

The main audience for this document is Information Technology (IT) staff wishing to carry out appraisals or evaluations for soundly based procurement.

This volume also will be of interest to senior IT management considering the introduction of Database Management products and wishing to ensure that such introduction is carried out professionally, resulting in the selection of the most appropriate product.

It is assumed that the reader has at least a basic understanding of data processing, the role of recommended standard methods such as PRINCE and SSADM and of hardware architecture. Knowledge of data management is not assumed, with introduction ii providing some background information and explanation of the terminology used in this volume.

Because of these assumptions experienced data management practitioners may find the volume too descriptive in some parts, but technically simplified in others. It should be remembered, however, that the document will be used as a primer by those unfamiliar with the topic, and also serving as a useful reference document for experienced people.

i.4 **Expected uses** It is expected that the volumes in this Library will be used in several ways. The uses identified in the Overview and Procedures Volume are:

- strategic, business-based, evaluation of products to select a 'standard' product for subsequent organisation-wide use

- less detailed evaluation of products as an element of a feasibility study

- full evaluation of products during procurement for a project

- independent appraisal of a product.

i.5 **Structure of this volume** This document is in three parts - introductions, the evaluation criteria and an annex.

This is the first introduction. Introduction ii describes the scope of the subject area and explains the terminology. Introduction iii describes the notation used for the criteria, and summarises the main headings.

The bulk of the volume contains the high level criteria and the checklists of detailed technical questions used within the evaluation model to assess and rank AG products. The questions can be used as an aide-memoire when gathering information about products.

The annex contains a hierarchy chart of the subject matter in this volume. This chart may be used as a default or as the basis for a hierarchy chart which best meets the needs of the project or organisation.

ISE Appraisal and Evaluation
Application Generators Volume

i.6 **Outline of the procedure**

The evaluation process comprises 7 stages which are described in the Overview and Procedures volume.

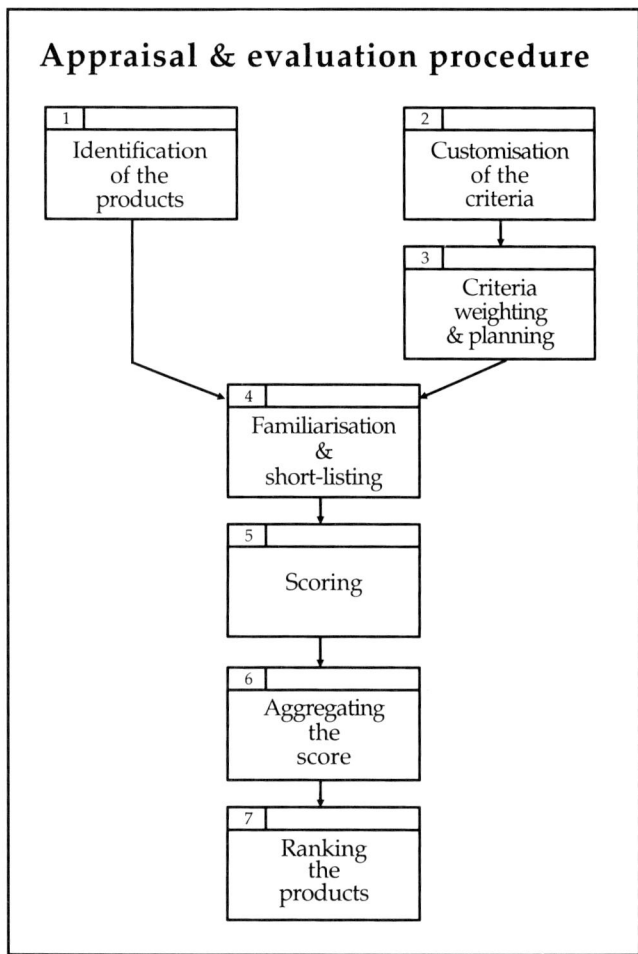

i.7 **History**

This AG volume supersedes ISE Report No. 32 - 'Application Generators - Appraisal and Evaluation', and the earlier report - 'Application Generator - Assessment Evaluation and Selection', published in 1988 and 1986 respectively. The content of this volume has been revised in the light of experience gained through being used in several major procurements and for technical appraisals of data management products. To make the volume easier to use detailed technical questions have been interspersed with the criteria.

ii Scope

ii.1 Scope of the volume

The evaluation criteria in this volume relate to Application Generator (AG) software products appropriate for the construction of multi user applications. The method is particularly suited to, and has been used on both strategic and tactical procurements (See the Overview and Procedures volume for further details).

ii.2 AG definition

The 'Data Management' arena can be very confusing for a beginner because of the multiplicity and contradictory nature of the terminology used by the product vendors and in the press. It is impossible to give a universally acceptable definition of terms such as '4GL' and '4GE'. New terms are invented frequently and new products are developed that transcend existing demarcations.

The term 'Application Generator' is used to refer to products that are capable of producing a wide variety of applications. The prime requirement of an Application Generator is the ability to develop applications in significantly less time and with significantly less comprehensive skill levels than by use of conventional programming.

Below is set out in a simple fashion, the definitions used in this volume. The fundamental distinction we can make is between the front-end application oriented elements and the back-end data management elements, with some form of data control or query language providing cohesion and integration. There is no necessity for the front and back-ends to come from the same vendor, indeed many vendors do not supply both.

Front-end

Typically the front-end will include several different elements used initially for developing applications and subsequently by the application when it is running. These elements may be grouped together and sold as a package, often collectively being called the 'Application Generator'(AG), or may be sold individually or in small groups. The complete front-end may alternatively be marketed as a Fourth

Generation Environment (4GE), or as a Fourth Generation System (4GS). Note that this Library classes the fourth generation language as a component of the AG - it is not unusual, however, to hear '4GL' being used as the collective term. Typical front-end tool elements are:

- forms - ability to design and construct screen images of forms (screens) which can be used for:

  - data entry into the database, and subsequent update, query, or deletion

  - help information

  - menu hierarchies.

  The forms facility often also allows the user to create and modify the database structure (often referred to as the Schema)

- Interactive Query Language - to enter directly data control language commands (see below)

- Fourth Generation Language (4GL) - usually a very high level language. Examples of these range from systems enabling complex form and report definition, menu control etc from within the 4GL; down to products containing little more than commands to control the flow through the processing code, and the ability to embed Query Language commands and access to forms, menus, etc

- 3GL Pre-Compilers - to enable query language commands, and sometimes forms, menus, and 4GL modules to be embedded in a third generation language such as COBOL, C or Fortran

- Report Writer - to extract data from the database and format it into structured reports. Often can also write data and thus provide batch functionality

- Data Dictionary - this can take many forms, from being the repository of data gathered during business analysis, system analysis and system specification. This information can be used for automatic system generation or simply be the directory or catalogue recording the database structure. The data dictionary itself usually utilises a data management back-end for the physical storage of its contents. Further tools such as Analysts' Workbenches provide access to the data dictionary

- Query Facility - to enable end users to formulate their own database queries. The Query Facilities may be:

  - forms based (see above)

  - Query-by-Example

  - a natural language interface

  - some method to aid the user in building a query language statement

- Decision Support Tools - facilities to draw graphs, or use spreadsheet like calculators, are available in some AGs.

While these tools may be bundled together some of them are more usually sold separately. This document does not include detailed criteria for Report Writers, Data Dictionaries, Query facilities, or Decision Support Tools.

The back-end also has several elements:

- Database Management System (DBMS)

- Distributed Processing

- Distributed Database.

Other back-end elements are available for tasks such as the bulk loading of data into the database, for importing or exporting data from a database, or for recovering the database after a failure. These may collectively form a set of database administrator utilities.

Ideally the back-end elements are transparent to the application and to the application developer. Only the database administrator (DBA) needs to know and understand them. (Having said that, knowledge of the underlying structure is advantageous to the developer in order to develop an efficient system and to tune it effectively.)

The front-end need not be on the same hardware as the back-end. Separation of the front-end application processing from the back-end DBMS processing is an essential aspect of distributed processing.

The data control or query language is used by the front-end elements to instruct the back-end elements. The two main elements of such a language are:

- data definition (DDL) - The DDL enables the database structure of files, indexes etc to be created and subsequently amended

- data manipulation (DML) - The DML allows data to be input, selected for display, updated, or deleted.

The query language will usually also have the ability to specify security and integrity factors that will govern the use of the DBMS.

ii.3 DBMS architectures

Database Management Systems are categorised by the way their data organisation may be visualised and manipulated:

- hierarchical

- network

- inverted list

- relational.

Hierarchical and Network types are the most widely used types of DBMSs on mainframe computers, Relational DBMSs, or RDBMSs, are relative newcomers. These are described in more detail in

Introduction ii
Scope

the DBMS Guide.

DBMS architecture is not a major consideration for AG appraisal, but the range of products with which an AG may interface may be constrained by the architecture assumed by the AG designer. The terminology defined below is an attempt to overcome the problem of duplicity of meanings between older and newer database architectures.

ii.4   **Terminology**

Products have evolved in different ways, consequently they have adopted different terminology for features that meet common objectives.

This chapter describes the terminology adopted in an endeavour to find a generally acceptable data management vocabulary.

The objective of an on-line application is to interact with the user in such a way that the user can efficiently carry out his job. The application will accept, process, store, and retrieve data. The user's job might be punching in data, requesting batch processed reports, or obtaining management information online by querying the database. The essence of all these is the application requesting some input, the user typing it in, and then sending it to the computer. We have used the term exchange to refer to this basic 'request, input and send' interaction.

An exchange, therefore, could be any one of the following:

- completion of a data entry form (screen)

- selection of an option from a menu

- cancellation of a help screen

- a single character response to a question, eg 'Accept (Y/N) >'

- sometimes completion of single fields on a form

- direct input of a query language command.

The collection of exchanges into a structure is referred to as the dialogue structure. Typically such a structure will contain menus, forms for data input and query, exchanges that cause reports to be printed or batch operations to be instigated, and often help screens that may be displayed. There also will be a convention as to the means by which the user can leave one exchange and go to another or to a menu, that is, generally move about within the dialogue structure provided, this is referred to as navigation.

Processing of the data may be required either before or after an exchange. We have referred to these as pre-map and post-map procedures.

iii Criteria

iii.1 Notation

The criteria in this document are structured as a hierarchy, this is illustrated in the annex.

The text is in three classes:

- the main discussion of the criteria - it is primarily this text that should be customised for particular projects against which weights are assigned and scores allotted. To obtain an overview of the criteria this text can be read in isolation. This is printed in 10 point Palatino typeface (ie the one used to print this volume) alongside a numbered heading in bold type, as in the top paragraph on this page. Where the criteria covers a large subject area it is divided into sub-criteria. This is printed in the normal typeface with an unnumbered side heading in the same typeface (ie not bolded)

- detailed discussion of the criteria or sub-criteria - this level is required for information gathering. This is also in the 10 point Palatino typeface, it does not have a heading

- *the supporting questions associated with the criteria or sub-criteria - these are in italics, as this example.*

iii.2 Summary of the criteria

The hierarchy of evaluation criteria against which application generators can be scored is summarised below and elaborated in the chapters that follow. A diagrammatic representation of the hierarchy adopted within this volume appears as an annex. It will, of course, be necessary to construct a hierarchy applicable to the needs of the project or organisation, which will more than likely be different to the one we have illustrated.

The top level criteria are:

- Generality - the types of applications that can be developed

- Usability - reflects overall productivity anticipated from the product and the skill levels required to use it

- Functionality - the range of functions provided by the product

- Integration with other System Products - degree of integration with major data management products which run in the same environment, for example a data dictionary

- Capability of System Components - total data management capability available to the user, from the AG or elsewhere

- Efficiency - machine resource usage for the development and production running of the applications

- SSADM Support and Tools - extent to which the product integrates with and supports the Government standard analysis and design methodology SSADM

- Quality Control Capability - of increasing importance for large projects. It applies in particular to the differences between 'tactical' and 'strategic' products

- Environment Independence - important if systems need to be moved to other environments

- End User Interface - ease of use and facilities available to the user

- Security - safety and control of access to the data

- Product Credibility - status of the product and supplier and degree of support

- Project Specific Criteria - other than above

- Costs.

It is expected that these criteria, with the exception of costs, will be weighted and scored as set out in the

Overview and Procedures volume of this library. The cost information will be required as an element of the selection procedure, or to exclude products from detailed consideration when they exceed planned budgets or cost ceilings.

Note that these criteria are not intended to form a tutorial on the subject under consideration. There is a wide range of published material available, including several reports and papers from CCTA. Please contact CCTA regarding the availability of appropriate documents.

iii.3 Questions

This volume consists of a discussion of each of the above criteria together with relevant detailed questions.

The questions should be used for familiarisation with a product before attempting to allocate scores against evaluation criteria.

Not all questions are relevant to all products, or projects, and they should be used selectively.

Experience has shown that little will be gained by having the vendor provide written answers to the questions. Only by probing can the evaluation team fully elicit the limits of the capabilities of the products. The best value will be obtained by attempting to answer questions after inspection of technical documentation and attending demonstrations.

ISE Appraisal and Evaluation
Application Generators Volume

1 Generality

The AG's generality is a measure of its functional capabilities. The AG's generality determines the scope of applications that can be developed.

1.1 On-line systems

To implement an on-line system the AG must be capable of constructing dialogues and exchanges. To define an exchange requires the ability to:

- define a non trivial pre-map process (ie processing to be undertaken prior to the display of an input screen of an exchange, to the application user). Here, non trivial implies the ability optionally to access multiple record types or record occurrences within the process in addition to normal processing such as arithmetic and conditional logic

- define the application screen format to be displayed and the data fields to be entered. There should be few or no restrictions

- define a non trivial post-map process (ie processing to be undertaken after results have been received from an input screen)

- update or access multiple record types or multiple record occurrences as a result of the exchange

- Decide by algorithm, directly or indirectly from the data input, the next exchange to be processed

- pass information between exchanges in order to allow the construction of multi exchange transactions.

Implicit within this definition is the concept of an on-line transaction success unit and the associated scope of the success unit.

Practicality

The majority of application generator products may be used to build on-line applications. This is because there is a general trend to develop new systems to operate primarily in an on-line rather than a batch mode. On-line systems tend to be simpler and more effective for the end user, moving control away from the computer department to the user.

Is the application generator intended to be used to build on-line systems?

File handling

Some application generators place restrictions on the number or the way in which files (or database record types in a database environment) can be handled. For example, an on-line process may allow for the update of one (hierarchically structured) database file only. This would have severe performance implications.

Some systems limit data access for an exchange to one file or record type (or even occurrence). While this is suitable for simple applications, general applications require more general file accessing capabilities.

From one screen (exchange), can the application

- *access more than one record of a particular type?*

- *update, create or delete more than one record of a particular type?*

- *access more than one type of record?*

- *update, create or delete occurrences of records of different types?*

- *access more than one file or type of file?*

- *update, create or delete occurrences of records within different files or files of different types?*

Screen handling

Some application generators do not contain screen definition facilities. They either use the operating system's screen definition facilities or they market them as a separate component.

Is the screen definition processor

- *a component of the application generator?*

Chapter 1
Generality

- *part of the host operating system?*

- *an additional purchasable component?*

Many application generators restrict screen design. If a new application is being constructed this could be worked round (as the business system design can recognise the constraints imposed by the software and avoid them). The restrictions may be a problem in a prototyping environment or where the requirement is to reimplement an existing system.

System defined screen message areas restrict the space available to the application.

Does the application have system generated screen headers, footers or message areas?

Most products restrict the representation of repeated fields to a tabular format.

In what formats can repeating fields be displayed?

General screen handling sophistication can be assessed by checking if the product can support all the facilities provided by terminal hardware (for example, highlighting, suppressing a character display, inverse video, etc).

Can the generator handle all the attributes you wish to use on the terminals you intend to use?

Restrictions on the way in which windows are handled; some products allow the programmer complete flexibility in handling windows. Other products may however restrict the format and scope of the window.

How does the generator handle windows, in particular placement, scrolling and sizing?

Variant screens are particularly useful in providing varying levels of help information on the screen, or to exclude knowledge of certain information from particular users. Using variant screens reduces the need to vary the application code for different users.

Can the screen definitions have variant forms to be used by different categories of users?

(See also chapter 10, 'End User Interface')

Communication areas

Some AGs limit the format or the amount of data that can be passed between business transactions. A temporary data storage area may be necessary to implement multi exchange business transactions. As this probably will be the only way of implementing a delayed file/database update, a relatively large area may be required.

Can data be passed from one exchange to another? If so, what are the restrictions on its size and format? Is the size and format under the control of the application specification or is it a system default?

Temporary data storage areas should be written to disc so that their contents may be used within system recovery.

Is the area used to pass data between exchanges recoverable in the event of a system failure?

Complexity restrictions

There may be significant restrictions in the complexity or nature of the processing statements within a pre-map or post-map procedure. If the application generator does impose significant restrictions, it is important to have the ability to escape into a lower level conventional language, possibly at the expense of usability.

If procedures cannot be directly associated with an exchange then possibly the only way of carrying out input validation, or ensuring referential integrity, may be coding in either a 4GL or a 3GL. If the exchange is used in more than one place consistency may be a problem. Note that some recent products place such procedural code in the DBMS to be either triggered automatically or be invoked by the AG.

Can pre-map and post-map procedures be associated with an exchange at the level of a screen or a field? What are the complexity restrictions on such use?

Chapter 1
Generality

Help facility
It should be possible to build a help facility for the end users, which can be invoked with a function key or some such mechanism from within an application. It should not be the responsibility of the application designer to have to devise the mechanism for providing this help information. For example field specific help text could be displayed on demand, or screens of textual information could be defined and chained together.

Can help screens be programmed?

Can help be context sensitive?

How much help can be accessed at all the various levels?

Multi user capability
While usually dependent on the capabilities of the underlying database management and transaction processing systems, some AG environments lack the concurrency control necessary to support multiple applications updating a common database. In particular, some systems on mini and micro computers claim to provide record level locking of data but their underlying architecture, being based on the host file system, allows only single record occurrences to be locked. In these cases it is possible to construct multi user systems but the design is more difficult and recovery is uncertain.

Is the application generator designed to support multiple concurrent users? How does it achieve this?

1.2 Batch systems

The characteristics of a batch system are that it can:

- be driven from a sequential input file containing 'business transactions'. This file could contain a single 'transaction' that initiates the production of a report. In such a case, the input transaction file would usually be referred to as a control file

- define batch business transaction boundaries (for recovery, integrity and performance purposes). Note however that the entire process may constitute a single 'transaction'

- perform non trivial user defined arithmetic, conditional or control operation sequences

- process (ie be able to read, optionally update, or create) multiple record types and multiple record occurrences within a batch business transaction

- produce printed output or reports in user specified formats.

Practicality

Several AGs are not capable of constructing batch systems. This is because AGs are generally more cost effective when used to build on-line applications. In such environments, purpose built report writer packages may give some support to the batch application requirements.

Is the application generator intended to be used to build batch systems?

Do batch applications run as independent programs or do they execute under some form of application generator runtime control routine?

Use of a 4GL or a 3GL is usually required in order to permit some form of control within the application.

How can batch applications be implemented?

It is desirable to be able to initiate a batch/background job from a generated on-line application. Having to use a job control language is not end user friendly.

Can batch applications be initiated:

- *via job control?*

- *from within a generated on-line application?*

- *from a host Transaction Processing system transaction?*

File handling

As for on-line systems, there should be no restrictions or limitations on the way in that files or databases

Chapter 1
Generality

can be handled. In particular, the ability to update several files or database record types is essential.

To provide a general batch capability it is necessary to have a general file handling capability.

Can a batch application:

- *access more than one record of a particular type?*

- *update, create or delete more than one occurrence of a record of a particular type?*

- *access more than one type of record?*

- *update, create or delete occurrences of records of different types?*

- *access more than one file or type of file?*

- *update, create or delete occurrences of records within different files or files of different types?*

Reporting

Not all products have comprehensive capabilities for defining report formats; this is analogous to restrictions on screen formats for on-line AGs.

Does the batch generator:

- *produce file/database update programs only?*

- *have report writing capability alone?*

- *produce output to a file/database for later processing by a report writer?*

Can a batch application produce reports on a printer from databases or files?

Complexity restrictions

Complex logic may need be to be used in developing the control structures and algorithms when building batch programs, the AG should not impose serious restrictions.

What control structures can be included in the batch application? Can additional processing, for example 3GL modules, be included?

29

Multi user capability — As for on-line systems, multi user capability is usually dependent on the facilities provided by the underlying database management system. However, it is necessary to be able to exploit the facilities provided by that software; in particular to be able to define success unit boundaries and to be able to predefined file or database area usage modes so that the DBMS can invoke the correct record locking strategies.

The ability to run batch and on-line applications concurrently on the same data probably depends on the features associated with the operating system and DBMS. Note that possibly even on-line applications might not have concurrent data access.

Can batch and on-line applications have concurrent access to the same databases (files)? If so, what facilities are provided to control concurrent access and maintain data integrity?

2 Usability

The ease of use of the product when developing applications is a major factor in determining the overall potential productivity level. This includes the ease of use of the application development tools, the learning curve and whether the tools can be used by end users to build their own enquiries.

2.1 Specification language

Specification type

AGs vary widely in the ways in which applications are specified. Extremes vary from a pure declarative approach through 'form filling' type languages to more conventional looking programming languages. These vary considerably in their usability and by whom they are capable of being used.

Form filling systems are more usable for inexperienced users. They are also probably preferable for prototyping.

What type of application specification language, or languages are available

- *declarative?*
- *form filling?*
- *3GL type?*

Suitability for non programmers

A potential advantage of the AG approach is that by removing the technical skill requirements from constructing applications, they can be constructed by analyst/programmers, thus avoiding the problems associated with the analyst producing program specifications for the programmer to code. While some AGs are to an extent usable by people with little formal programming training, others require conventional programming skills. DP skills are however still necessary to understand the concepts of good system design etc.

What elements of the product can be used by people without DP skills?

What elements of the product can be used by analysts?

Do any elements of the product require a knowledge of programming?

Do any elements of the product require a knowledge of database design?

Batch/on-line system specification compatibility	The language, syntax and system development environment for constructing and testing batch systems should be identical to on-line systems so minimising programmer training and support overheads.

Is the same language and development environment used to specify both batch and on-line applications?

2.2 Application development tools

The usability of tools available to the application developers can significantly affect their productivity.

Specification editor

The minimum requirement is a purpose designed 'full screen' editor or editors for screens, program code, administration details etc, with the movement between them being transparent to the user. If the application takes the form of a series of program like statements, sophisticated editors make the program writing easier, quicker and much less prone to errors. A sophisticated program editor should allow short codes to be used for standard constructs and prompt the user by automatically inserting complete construct skeletons. This allows the system to maintain a neat, indented program layout. It also allows the user to manipulate entire program constructs rather than individual lines or symbols.

Own, purpose built editors are usually the most user friendly. Using host operating system or dictionary editors usually implies switching to another environment to edit an application specification.

How is the application specification maintained:

- *host operating system file editor?*

- *data dictionary editor?*

Chapter 2
Usability

- *application generator's own editor(s)?*
- *other (please specify)?*

Does the editor automatically provide construct skeletons?

Line and context based editors are the least user friendly. Full screen editors are most suitable for 'expert' mode working. Formatted screens are best for novice users. Note that it is possible that a generator will include more than one editor, or that the user may make his own choice of editor.

Is the editor used to maintain the application specification

- *line based?*
- *context based?*
- *'full screen' based?*
- *based on the use of formatted screens?*

Does the system present a seamless interface to the user?

If not how does the generator provide editing facilities to the user?

Where more than one editor is used, is the movement between editors transparent?

Can the user make his own choice of editor?

Some systems completely separate specification maintenance from compilation. Interactive syntax checking helps to correct errors early.

Does the product's application specification editor (or data entry system) include interactive syntax checking?

Screen definition

When a screen has been defined, it is important to be able to edit the definition without unnecessary respecification. Some packages make a poor attempt at screen painting, using marker characters and optional field coordinates.

A significant difficulty with screen painting is the specification of the multitude of attributes and field names required. One way is to split the screen into two windows, with part of the users screen image in one window and a 'fill in the blanks' formatted screen in the other, an alternative is to have pop-up windows that appear as required.

If the screen definition is within the application then it is probably not easy to have common screens in several exchanges. If the host system's screen definition facilities are used then this probably means either having to learn another language or having to move from one development environment to another during an application specification.

How are the application's screens defined

- *interactively, using a 'paint the screen' technique?*
- *by drawing the layout in a text editor?*
- *by specifying field names and coordinates on pre formatted help screens?*
- *by specifying field names and coordinates within the application definition?*
- *by specifying field names and coordinates in the screen definition language of the host system?*
- *any other method?*

How are attributes specified?

Screen painting alone is acceptable in a prototyping environment, but for production work it is necessary to be able to edit the screen definitions for consistency.

If a screen painting technique is used, can the definition be edited?

To establish whether the screen definition exists as a separate application independent entity for use in more than one place.

Can one screen definition be used by multiple applications?

Chapter 2
Usability

When defining a screen, it also should be possible to declare the validation rules, error messages and other pre-map and post-map functionality. Ideally validation should be held centrally to be enforced globally. Particular local constraints also may apply. Local error messages are important because differently skilled users may use different parts of the application.

Can validation rules, error messages and calls to other procedures be associated with individual fields or complete screens? How complex can this be?

2.3 Application testing

AG produced applications, like conventionally produced applications, need to be developed and tested in chapters as the application specification may contain errors. To achieve high productivity, an AG must include testing and debugging aids.

Prototyping

In order to prototype the application it is necessary to produce a dialogue that at a minimum appears to function.

Prototyping is a useful facility to demonstrate to a user what a system is likely to look like (at the exchange/dialogue level).

Can menu hierarchies be quickly and easily implemented?

Do facilities exist for linking and displaying screen sequences before writing application code?

'Screen painting' is useful in a prototyping mode. If the screen definition is within the application then it is probably not very easy to have common screens in several exchanges.

How are the application's screens defined?

- *interactively, using a 'paint the screen' technique*
- *by drawing the layout using a text editor*
- *by specifying field names and coordinates on preformatted help screens*

- *by specifying field names and coordinates within the application definition*

- *by specifying field names and coordinates in the screen definition language of the host Transaction Processing system.*

If screens cannot be displayed immediately (say they require compilation) the AG is less suitable for working directly with a user.

Does the screen definition require compilation before it can be displayed?

If the screen is defined using field coordinates, can the screen be displayed immediately?

Systems which use the host system's run time screen mapping facilities (and therefore invariably generate screen definition source language statements) are usually less suited to a rapid development/prototyping environment.

Does the screen definition process include generating source statements in the host system's screen definition language, followed by having to compile this definition?

Some systems will only pick up a new screen or program when they are restarted. For others, the program and screen format libraries are dedicated and cannot be updated. Such restrictions make rapid development in a prototyping environment difficult.

Does the system normally have to be brought down or restarted

- *to include revised screen formats?*
- *to include new screen formats?*
- *to include revised applications?*
- *to include new applications?*

Incremental testing
To allow incremental testing of an application, it is desirable for the AG to provide sensible defaults for

as yet unspecified attributes. If an unspecified module is invoked, the system enters 'test' mode, allows the tester to emulate the results of the module by adjusting variable values, and continues. Another approach is to allow program statements or segments to be executed immediately in isolation, but this is less convenient than the 'defaults' approach.

It is highly desirable that parts of an application can be tested in isolation, usually before other parts are developed.

Can applications be developed incrementally using a top down design philosophy (ie allowing testing with an incomplete application specification)?

Can application elements be invoked independently?

Can individual application specification statements be executed on entry? If so, can such a sequence of executed statements be saved to form part of an application specification?

Debugging

In order to locate errors, it is helpful if the AG contains some facilities to enable the run to be monitored or logged. Most products are weak in this area, requiring that the application specification be modified to obtain debugging trace information.

What facilities (please state whether interactive or not) exist for runtime debugging of

- *on-line applications?*

- *batch applications?*

Systems could attempt to test for completeness by ensuring that all process inputs and outputs are compatible. Most systems do not really address this area.

What facilities exist for checking the consistency and completeness of the system specification? Which of these facilities are interactive?

2.4 Development environment

It is desirable that the AG may be used effectively without a significant programmer learning overhead and that applications can be developed and tested with minimal delays.

Components

Ideally, the user of an AG should only be required to master a single environment, which has all the facilities he needs.

How many different components does the product have (i.e. screen painter, menu builder etc)?

How many different approaches does the developer need to learn before a complete system can be created, ie is a screen developed in the same way that a menu or report would be?

Environment type

There are a wide range of types of development environment, and the best type for one group of users is not necessarily the best for another group.

Mouse driven and menu driven environments are easiest to use and therefore suitable for novices, whereas command driven are the quickest to use by experts.

Is the application development environment menu driven, command driven, or a combination of the two?

Is a mouse driven environment available?

Some application generators generate applications in COBOL or another third generation language. Ideally an application can be tested interactively and then either be compiled or generated.

Is the application generated, compiled, or interpreted? Can more than one option be used?

Some systems generate code in a range of languages. A standard language is desirable.

What languages can be generated? Do these comply with international standards?

Integration of editing and compiling

Where a specification needs to be compiled, it should be possible to initiate the compilation from the development environment (for example from within a specification editor); the developer should not be required to master the intricacies of job control languages or compiler steering lines.

Is the compiler or generator invoked:

- *directly from the application specification maintenance subsystem?*

- *using job control?*

Some generators always produce the entire system in a single generation run. For large systems this can take a considerable time and is not suitable in a large or volatile system environment.

What is the smallest component of the application system that can be separately generated?

- *entire systems*

- *single on-line transaction or batch program*

- *other (please specify).*

The unit of generation is not necessarily the same as the unit of compilation. Ideally it should be possible to recompile individual transactions (exchanges or batch programs).

What is the smallest component that can be separately compiled?

- *entire system*

- *single on-line transaction or batch application*

- *other.*

It is desirable that the user has some control over when recompilation takes place.

If the application specification is modified, is the application recompiled:

- *automatically at the next program execution?*

- *when directed by the user?*

- *at the completion of the edit of the specification?*
- *other?*

Speed of compilation turnaround

It is desirable that any compilation be quick so that the application is rapidly available for testing. Ideally, this implies operating in a foreground (ie real-time) environment in order to obtain a rapid response. AGs which allow the rapid development of the application, but then require systems programmer action to link the application to the database and/or transaction processing monitor are not productive. These options may be selectable by the developer. What is used may be dependent on the machine resource available.

Are compilations run in a real-time environment?

Is any non real-time processing involved before an application can be tested in an application system environment?

Development help information

At any stage of development it should be possible to obtain on-line help information; this facility is especially useful after the system has generated an unfamiliar error message. Several products now provide this facility. Some allow on-line access to the manual in a help mode.

Are help screens available as part of a comprehensive help system?

Batch and/or on-line application specification

While applications usually will be developed on-line, it may on occasions be desirable to have the option of developing them (ie specifying and testing them) in a batch mode. Several products allow the specification, but not the testing of applications.

Can the generator operate as a batch or pseudo-batch job?

Quality of generation

Where code in a third generation language is generated it is important that it should be to a high quality.

Chapter 2
Usability

One of the quoted advantages of a source language generator approach is that the code is easily maintainable.

Can the generator be constrained to produce code that conforms to recognised programming language standards?

What documentation, if any, is generated?

The form in which programs are generated can have an effect on machine performance.

Are the generated programs reentrant, reusable or single thread only?

Some systems generate a single, very large application load module element - this is undesirable. Ideally the system designer should be able to fragment the load module so that the fragmentation is not apparent to the end user.

What control does the application developer have over the maximum size of the resultant application load modules?

If a data dictionary is not being used then it is necessary to separate development and production (object) libraries. Ideally the user should be able to nominate where the object code will be saved.

If the application is compiled, where is the object code placed and what control does the user have over placement?

Many of the interpretive systems semicompile their code. The vendors frequently claim them to be 'compiled' systems.

Is the resultant object code the machine code for the target machine?

2.5 Data and application definition

Most application generators make significant use of globally maintained data and file definitions; this avoids the need to respecify. However, restrictions on the use of these definitions affect the products usability.

Flexibility of global definitions	While centrally stored global definitions are useful, frequently it is necessary to override locally a global definition (for example for specific field validation or edit rules).
	For some applications different validation rules, or slightly different screen layouts, may be required in different parts of the application.
	Can definitions be stored centrally for global use? If so can these global definitions be overwritten locally in part to provide local variants?
	The same user, at different times, or different users, may require a different view of the data at the same point in the application. For example the layout of a screen may change, or certain fields and their prompts may be suppressed for security reasons.
	Can one definition, say of a screen, be stored with multiple variants?
Element specification procedure	It should be possible to specify elements (ie files, fields, processes etc) without regard to the order of specification (although it is accepted that some entry time checking will not be available if other elements are not defined). Products where the elements need to be specified in a strict order are not helpful; they necessitate analysts and designers working with paper when the dictionary should be a better, more productive vehicle. In addition, with such restrictions, changes to definitions become more time consuming.
	Do the files, fields, exchanges and processes need to be defined in a set order, or can the developer impose his own construction sequence?

3 Functionality

The functionality of the product in developing applications is a major factor in determining the overall potential productivity level of the development process and the resultant application. Tools that can build powerful constructs enable the application to be built quickly and enable the end user to access data efficiently.

3.1 Specification storage

The mechanism by which the application specification is stored will affect the functionality of the tools using it. Note that this subject may be covered by a separate Data Dictionary appraisal.

Application specifications stored in simple file or database structures can usually be modified with a variety of editors, etc. For larger, more complex applications some form of dictionary is desirable. Application generators' own dictionaries are frequently unsuitable for general dictionary purposes unless they have been designed as comprehensive complementary products.

How is the application specification stored?

- *host operating system file*
- *conventional database file*
- *host operating system library file*
- *application generator's own file system*
- *application generator's own data dictionary system*
- *proprietary data dictionary system (please specify)*
- *other (please specify).*

3.2 Specification language

AGs vary widely in the ways in which applications are specified. Extremes vary from a pure declarative approach, through 'form filling' type languages, to more conventional looking programming languages.

Suitability for programmers	The type of specification language used affects the experience profile requirements of the target application developers and the likely acceptability of the product, especially by professional programmers. Some products contain constructs which are likely to be familiar to professional programmers, others are usable by less experienced programmers (frequently at the expense of generality or completeness). In general menu driven, form filling or application specification languages of very simple appearance, are more likely to encounter programmer resistance on the grounds that the building of applications is not 'programming'.
	Some products generate parts of programs, rather than complete application systems. These may be termed program generators rather than application generators. Note, however, that most generators allow the inclusion of conventional code for exceptional processing. Some specification languages lack the required functionality to perform all the processing required.
	Can the entire application be written in the specification language, or is it usual or necessary to use a conventional programming language for parts of the application?
	Whilst a good application generator specification language is capable of specifying most commercial applications completely, there is always the possibility that some special process will require conventional programming techniques (eg unpacking data formats not supported by the generator). Commercial generators should support standard languages.
	Is it possible to specify the invocation of subroutines or procedures written in a conventional programming language from within an application? If so, which languages are supported?
Style and quality	Good, well designed languages have few irregularities or exceptional rules for the programmer to contend with. Some products are close enough to conventional languages to be easily mastered by programmers, others have specification languages based on different concepts such as set based constructs which some conventional programmers

may find hard to adjust to. Non programmer languages are usually more rigid in what they allow the developer to write. A variety of approaches have been adopted for specifying applications, short annotated examples of actual applications should be sought. Examples taken from training manuals will usually be satisfactory.

Please describe the style and quality of the application specification language, using examples if this is beneficial?

Data sublanguage

Application Generators are most often used with Database Management Systems. The AG will use a data sublanguage (for data definition and data manipulation) to interact with the DBMS. This is described in detail in Chapter 4.2 below.

4 Integration with other products

It may often be necessary for an AG to interface to other data management products that are possibly being installed as part of the same project. These products may alternatively have been installed as part of a departmental strategy or standard, or the AG may be required to extend an existing application that uses other products.

The ability to interact with other products reduces the possibility of having to install software that duplicates existing capability. It is likely to be cheaper in hardware and software terms than separate environments.

AGs are marketed as:

- single packaged products with integrated data management capability

- part of an 'Integrated Product Range' from a single supplier, with the individual components within the range sold as separate products

- having interfaces to host system data management software.

Where products need to interact with other components, the interaction is particularly important with respect to:

- data dictionary

- DBMS

- transaction processing monitor.

Note that if separate appraisals of other components are being undertaken then the integration aspects may need to be considered in isolation because of the multiplexity of combinations that may be possible.

4.1 Integration with data dictionary

Application generators, almost without exception, use some form of dictionary or directory as a repository for system specification information. The role of a data dictionary and the need for an AG to use centralised element definition, make it desirable that the AG and other parts of the organisation use the same dictionary. The sophistication of the interface between the AG and the dictionary affects the product's usability and the ability to audit and control system development.

Some products maintain their own specific dictionary giving the organisation the problem of maintaining consistency between two different, non compatible dictionary systems. Some vendors have software bridges to overcome this problem.

Other vendors have powerful dictionary products with close interfaces to the AG products. They are capable of supporting both analysis and implementation details and allow the dictionary meta structure to be extended to cater for local requirements.

Linkage, through a dictionary, to data produced by microcomputer based analysts workstations is likely to become an important factor in the future.

User sites will frequently have a considerable investment in a proprietary data dictionary system and will wish to use the same system to document (at least in parts) generated applications.

If the application specification is not stored within a conventional proprietary data dictionary, is bridging software available to relate the application specification to a proprietary data dictionary? If so, which dictionaries and how?

4.2 Integration with DBMS

If the requirement is to use a host DBMS, the code produced by the AG must be capable of utilising and exploiting the facilities provided by that DBMS to support recovery and integrity and to provide usability and functionality. Many products do not have a particularly close interface with alien database management systems. This may be significant for those projects considering using open systems interfaces. Interworking may be possible but fall short of well integrated, easy to use facilities. For example, it may be necessary with some products to

Chapter 4
Integration with other products

write interface code in a conventional language to perform functions like opening and closing a database and to handle the mapping between database records and the record structure used by the application generator.

Standards conformance

The selection of an AG and DBMS that both conform to ANSI and ISO international standards will greatly aid integration.

Will the AG utilise and/or exploit the facilities offered by a host DBMS from a different source? Does the AG conform with any of the international standards?

Database and file definition

Database and file definition is usually carried out by using the DBMS tools, or by using a Data Definition language. Definition from within the AG can be beneficial.

The application must clearly know of the database/record structure. Ideally this should be held in a dictionary/directory. Some systems describe the data structure as part of the application so that if the structure changes all applications using the structure require amendment. Some systems deduce a database structure from the application screen layouts.

Is the database or file definition provided as part of the application specification

- *explicitly?*
- *implicitly?*
- *not part of the application specification?*

If the DBMS and the application generator are integrated they should use the same definition. If they are not integrated it is useful if the database definition need be specified/coded only once.

Is the database or file definition used by the application specified in the same language as the database or file description used by the DBMS?

If the application specification implicitly produces the database definition it is probable that the user has little or no capability to tune the structure.

Can the same file or database specification be used by more than one application?

Is the database definition separate from the application specification?

If the file or database definition is derived from or contained within the application specification, what facilities exist:

- *for tuning the database structure?*

- *for reorganising the database structure?*

Most application generators support only a small subset of conventional data types.

What data formats are supported and what are the restrictions on their size?

Data field input and output

Data validation can be specified in many ways. For consistency it is best stored with the data item definition for global use. It is preferable if the validation rules can be input via the AG.

Where validation rules can be specified at the data item definition level they need not be inserted into every application.

Can the following field input validations be defined for a data item?

- *field is all numeric*

- *field is all alphabetic characters*

- *field is mandatory*

- *field lies within specified ranges*

- *field exists within specified list of values*

- *field is cross validated with other fields*

- *other.*

Chapter 4
Integration with other products

There should be default actions.

What action occurs if an input field fails one of the validation checks?

Can default actions on input be defined?

What data output representations can be specified when defining a data item:

- *default column headings?*

- *default size (different from storage size)?*

- *edited output representation (please indicate how the output representation is specified)?*

Data, file and database accessing facilities

The AG may be part of an integrated product range, it may use only standard system files, or it may be sufficiently flexible to access a range of DBMS products. This requirement will be dependent on the project environment.

Some systems are primarily designed to interface to their own DB system. They do, however, handle other database structures, but in read only mode. Frequently when an application generator is able to process an alien database structure it does not support all of the DBMS' capabilities.

Is the application generator primarily associated with the vendor's own database system?

What other files and database systems may be accessed?

What restrictions are imposed when accessing data from other systems?

- *read only*

- *limits on the structured complexity of the database*

- *database or file features or operations not supported.*

Applications generators usually support a small number of data representations. Conversion is usually by a conventionally coded interface routine. If the generator is to be introduced into an existing environment the inability to handle general database structures produced for conventionally coded (existing) applications is a severe limitation.

Can the generated application access files and databases previously created for conventionally programmed applications? If so, how are data types converted when they are not supported by the application generator program?

A 'CALL' type interface is necessary if conventional applications are to access the data held in the DB component of the application generator system. If such an interface does not exist applications will be 'locked in' to the AG system even if efficiency is a problem.

If the application generator is primarily associated with its own database system, how can the data be processed realistically by conventionally produced applications?

4.3 Integration with transaction processing system

In some environments the development of large or complex computer systems is likely to necessitate the use of advanced transaction processing (TP) monitor facilities for performance reasons. This chapter only applies to this type of system.

Few AGs have these facilities built in, so it is often required to use some host TP monitor. In order to make the best use of its facilities, the AG needs to be well integrated with the TP monitor. In addition, the degree of integration at the interface level affects the usability of the AG.

Application integration

For high performance applications it is essential that the application be well integrated into a TP environment.

Can the application run in a TP environment? Does it make full use of the TP monitor facilities?

How well is the application integrated into the TP environment?

Development environment integration

To develop an application to run under a TP monitor it is possible that the development environment will also need to utilise one.

Chapter 4
Integration with other products

Can the development environment run under a TP monitor? Is it necessary to produce a TP application?

To what extent is the development environment well integrated into the TP environment?

Recovery

Recovery is usually managed by DBMS rather than the AG. When this is not so, coordinated DB/TP recovery is necessary. It is probably acceptable if the generator uses a host DB/TP system. This may not be the case if the generator contains its own DB system.

For on-line systems, is database and TP recovery coordinated?

Does the application generator contain its own terminal/message handler? If so, what information is logged automatically for recovery purposes?

- all system accesses
- all input messages
- all successful transactions
- all output messages
- other (please specify).

Does utility software exist to enable messages to be reprocessed?

4.4 Integration with operating system

Recovery

Recovery for multi exchange business transactions is required if general systems are to be constructed. Ideally, it should use a DB provided delayed update technique. Some systems provide their own facilities to enable the user to directly manipulate temporary data storage areas. Minicomputer based systems may require the user to create a small temporary file for the life of the transaction. Note that any such temporary data storage area should be recoverable.

Does the AG rely on the underlying DBMS for recovery?

If the AG does not rely on the underlying DBMS for recovery does it support recovery for multi exchange business transactions? If so, are database updates performed using:

- *DBMS handled delayed update technique?*

- *application generator handled delayed update technique (using the temporary data storage area)?*

- *application handled delayed update technique (the application specification saving data within the temporary data storage area or other files)?*

- *locked database records across exchanges?*

Does the application generator contain its own data file handling routines? What information is logged automatically for recovery purposes

- *before images?*

- *after images?*

- *database transactions?*

- *other (please specify)?*

What utilities exist to facilitate database recovery?

For batch applications, is checkpointing or any other recovery technique supported?

If only simple use of DB/TP recovery services is made, recovery probably will be to the last (completed) exchange. In many systems (especially secure ones) this will not be sufficient - the operator may have left the terminal when it becomes live again. Ideally the application should be able to decide the recovery state.

In the event of a system failure during an on-line application, will the user's terminal be recovered to

- *the end of the last (completed) exchange?*

- *the start of the dialogue?*

- *the logon sequence only?*

- *a point determined by the application design? (for example start of business transaction).*

5 Capabilities of other system components

When assessing software for a project, it is not reasonable to assess the capabilities of an application generator in isolation from the capabilities of other components of system software. This is true irrespective of whether the components are supplied as separate products, or as part of the AG. Other major system components are:

- data dictionary
- DBMS
- TP monitor
- report writer
- query language/processor.

This document does not attempt to undertake a detailed evaluation of all these components. Instead, a single score is attributed to each. The derivation of this score is not covered here but is likely to involve an exercise similar to the evaluation of AGs. Criteria for the assessment of DBMS are given in the Database Management Systems volume of this library.

5.1 Capabilities of data dictionary

Good data dictionary facilities are usually regarded as central to effective documentation and control; this applies to AG and non AG developed systems.

While most AGs include some form of data dictionary capability, this is frequently unusable for non AG applications.

Can the data dictionary be used for non AG development?

It is important that the metadata in the dictionary can be accessed in an ad hoc manner to produce additional reports required by the analyst. This can be best achieved if the data dictionary has been developed using tools available to the analyst to extend the dictionary if required ie it has been implemented using an AG and DBMS.

Is the Data Dictionary implemented as a database that can be accessed by standard DBMS tools?

Does the dictionary tool set include a range of standard reports?

The dictionary should be capable of holding more than just the data definition. Additional detail is required for full support of analysis, and potentially for automatic systems generation.

Does the dictionary support process as well as data definition?

Does the dictionary support the business model as well as the application model?

5.2 Capabilities of DBMS

The facilities of a DBMS are a mandatory requirement to support multiple updating users in an on-line environment. Some products are not supported by proper DBMS software despite the claims of the vendors. Suspect areas are usually insufficient support of concurrency control or recovery in a multi user environment.

Is the AG supported by a fully functioning DBMS? How does the DBMS support concurrency control and recovery in a multi user environment?

5.3 Capabilities of the TP monitor

In some environments a TP monitor will be required to control terminals and the service and for recovery purposes. Special support is required to handle multi phase (multi exchange) business transactions, as communication areas may need to be preserved, and database records locked, over several exchanges. Very few products are able to do this.

In cases where there is a choice, a product that uses a TP monitor is likely to give better performance than one that does not.

Can the AG be used with a TP monitor? Are the TP monitor, or the AG, restricted in any way when used together?

Chapter 5
Capabilities of other system components

5.4 Capabilities of report writer

Report writing is a significant part of most batch applications. Real applications often demand complex reports. Good report writers, by enabling that function to be separated, simplify the system and give useful productivity gains.

General information - note that field/coordinate type specification is the least usable. The use of a separate report writing package may imply that the application generator produces a separate intermediate database/file.

Does the application generator include a report specification facility?

How are report formats specified?

- *interactively using 'screen painting' techniques*
- *by specifying field names and coordinates on pre formatted help screens*
- *by specifying field names and coordinates within the application*
- *by specifying field names and coordinates to a separate report writing package*
- *other (please specify).*

'Screen painting' is good when working directly with the user, but usually the definition requires editing later for consistency. It is undesirable to have to repaint the screen to effect minor changes. When working directly with a user it is desirable to be able to show them the report layout quickly.

If a 'screen painting' technique is used, can the definition be edited?

If the report is defined using field coordinates, can the report layout be displayed immediately?

General questions on report writer's capability.

Does the report exist as a separate entity independent from the application specification?

Can the report specification be used within multiple applications?

Can report output be directed to the VDU initially during development and then to a printer for production operation?

What options exist for sorting the data to be reported?

Can ascending or descending key sequences be specified?

What is the maximum number of sort keys that can be specified?

Can ascending and descending sequences be intermixed?

Can control breaks be specified? If so, what is the maximum number?

What facilities exist for totalling and other computation?

Is it necessary to specify field formats or column headings within the report specification? If not, from where are the defaults obtained?

Can default field formats or column headings be overridden in specific instances?

Can graphs, histograms, pie charts and other graphical representations be produced?

It may be desirable to produce more than one report from one pass of a file for efficiency and integrity (of results) reasons.

What is the maximum number of reports that can be produced from one pass of the data?

5.5 Capabilities of query facility

The increased requirement from end users to be able to access data directly means that some form of powerful query facility is frequently required to augment the purpose built application constructed with an AG. Note that many query languages are particularly friendly for unskilled end users.

Major DBMS products are associated with Report Writers and Query Languages. AGs built on such products are likely to meet most requirements in both areas.

Chapter 5
Capabilities of other system components

Are queries expressed

- *using a formatted help screen?*

- *using a relational or set based language?*

- *other (please specify)?*

Does the Application Generator include a query language facility?

Does the query language adhere to the SQL international standard? If not does it adhere to any other generally accepted standards? Please specify which standard.

Can individual query language statements be executed interactively?

Some systems differentiate between their own file systems (which are supported) and alien file types that are not.

Does the query language facility operate with all the file or database structures supported by the application generator? If not, which are not supported?

A join type facility within queries is necessary for all but the most simple application systems.

Are queries restricted to single files only?

General information - note that systems using a formatted help type screen will possibly have a second interface for direct use within applications.

Does the user have to know the files in which the data items reside or is the information held within a dictionary/directory?

Are the records or fields retrieved as a result of executing one query saved and available to be used in further queries?

What facilities are available to assist the end user to formulate queries?

What facilities are available to make the breaking down of complex queries easier?

Can retrieved data be formatted for presentation using the report writer facilities?

Can graphs, histograms, pie charts and other graphical representations be produced?

6 Efficiency

One of the primary objectives in purchasing of AG is to reduce the time taken to develop applications.

In achieving this AGs necessarily consume a high level of resources, both during development and In production use The performance/efficiency factors are usually of major importance.

It is also important to be aware that the measurement of the efficiency of an AG may not be simply a matter of measuring CPU resources used. Other metrics include:

- Memory usage - some systems are not effectively multithreaded, and so require significant storage resources

- I/O activity - systems claiming on-line interactions with a dictionary usually generate much I/O activity.

When an organisation acquires an AG, it frequently acquires other advanced software such as a DBMS. Such software is usually resource intensive in its own right.

6.1 Development productivity

Vendors claim significant productivity gains for their products over conventional 3GL development. It must be stressed that these gains only pertain to a small element of the system life cycle, namely application design, and that use of an AG does not remove the need for thorough systems analysis. Secondly a large proportion of any gain can be lost by iterating the design.

It is essential that any gains can be verified by contacting users of the product.

What productivity gains have been objectively measured by reference sites over the use of a 3GL such as COBOL or PL/1?

6.2 Development resource usage

Most AG development work is carried out on-line and response time and therefore machine efficiency are important to maintain the productivity of application developers. While application development is principally a one off activity compared with the application being run in a production mode, it is desirable that not too many resources are used. In particular, compilers for AGs can be large. Also, because the normal method of working is to develop small sections of code, to test and debug them, and then to proceed, it is desirable that the application can be compiled/interpreted in small units.

The development resource requirement is often greater than for runtime of the developed end application. It may be that the project will have to accept slower development, or shift working, to fit hardware constraints. The requirement is also often greater than the vendor would care to admit, again reliable reference site contacts are vital.

What hardware configuration is required (in terms of RAM and Disc Memory etc) to support the proposed number of application developers? Can this be verified by reference sites?

6.3 Runtime resource usage

Efficiency of machine resource usage for the developed application affects the type of application for which the product will be suitable. Interpretive implementations are usually less efficient than compiled implementations. This is no disadvantage in low transaction rate, test or prototyping environments. It is a serious disadvantage if high transaction rates are to be supported. Few products claim to be able to execute the same specification either interpretatively or from compiled code. A desirable additional requirement is the ability to invoke low level code on occasions for particularly performance critical sections of applications.

Runtime usage is heavily dependent on the performance of the underlying DBMS and its query optimiser.

Chapter 6
Efficiency

Separating the AG and DBMS processing loads into a client/server architecture can give considerable performance gains.

Can the application front end be run on separate processor from its DBMS? Can this front end be a workstation for each user?

Can more than one application front end be supported?

Is there an algorithm to estimate the resource requirements for each user? Is there a minimum memory requirement for each user?

7 Structured Systems Analysis and Design Methodology

The use of SSADM is widespread in both private and public sectors. These users do not wish to introduce a different range of techniques and procedures for each Application Generator they use because that would compromise their standards, reduce protection of investment and generally increase long term costs.

With this in mind CCTA has recommended to government departments that they contractually require suppliers to provide guidelines on how best to use their products with SSADM. This guidance should address all aspects of the product, including documentation and training The detailed objective of this CCTA policy is to:

- reinforce the fact that analysis and logical design still need to be conducted rigorously and in a controlled way, even when AGs are used for implementation

- allow a smooth transition from logical to physical design without gaps, duplication or damaging compromise of requirements

- make full use of SSADM requirements and design deliverables - particularly in a turnkey or facilities management situation

- produce good quality documentation for the maintenance, future enhancement and eventual replacement of the system.

SSADM is presented and documented as an integrated set of structural, technical and documentation standards. The assessment of supplier support for their product in a project using SSADM should be assessed against all three sets of standards.

7.1 Compatibility

The rigour of SSADM should not be compromised and the following section explores the extent to which the AG suppliers guidance is compatible with SSADM.

The purpose of the SSADM Analysis phase is to analyse and document the user requirement without the constraints imposed by any particular implementation choices. This logical view is enshrined in the following techniques, which should not be changed for use with the AG

- Data Flow Diagramming (DFD)

- Logical Data Structuring (LDST)

- Security, Control and Audit (SCA)

- User Options (USOP)

- Entity Life Histories (ELH)

- Relational Data Analysis (RDA)

- Composite Logical Data Design (CLDD).

Does the AG supplier provide guidelines on how to implement the application following on from the SSADM logical design?

Is there a tailored form of the SSADM Task List to lead the practitioner through the method, in a way compatible with the NCC Reference Manual indicating which SSADM tasks can be undertaken using the AG and any modified techniques?

The guidance should describe the use of standard SSADM end products and techniques with the modified techniques and end products designed to maximise the usefulness of the AG. The guidance will be of little value if it cannot be quality assured with the standard SSADM document set.

Are there supporting descriptions of the cross referencing and quality assurance of the modified end products to assist the smooth and effective operation of SSADM Reviews?

Although SSADM is a prescriptive method, and CCTA recommend that the components listed above are not altered, it is a flexible method. The ways in which that flexibility can be exploited by the guidance available from AG suppliers are principally as follows:

- Logical dialogue design (LDD)
- Process Outlines (PO)
- First Cut Data Design (DD)
- Program Specification (PS)
- Physical Design Control (PDC).

Does the guidance on On-line Process design include

- *logon/logoff screen designs?*
- *menu specifications?*
- *menu screen specifications?*
- *process descriptions, extended for dialogue context?*
- *specification of retrievals?*

Does the guidance for Dialogue Design include

- *dialogue screen designs, control tables and step definitions?*
- *both basic and full logical dialogue structures (The latter show to commit strategy)?*

Does the guidance for Dialogue Navigation include

- *how variable commit strategies are defined?*
- *how redisplay, either in the same or a restarted session is specified?*

Does the guidance on Batch Process Design include

- *input and output formats?*
- *transient file design?*
- *logical and physical process descriptions and structures?*
- *physical process specifications?*

- *specifications of retrievals?*
- *description of the front end processing of the input stream?*

First Cut Data Design rules define the mapping of the logical data design to a physical implementation, and this may need to be done in practice as part of the Technical Options activity, as well as in physical design. In physical design, the design is tested against performance objectives, and tuned. Suppliers are well placed to provide these rules.

Is there a set of First Cut Data Design rules, and if not, what is to be done?

Is guidance available on tuning the data design?

SSADM is an evolving standard and suppliers of AGs should be prepared to commit themselves to supporting new versions as and when they become available.

Does the AG supplier intend to support future versions of SSADM?

7.2 Tool support of SSADM

If an analyst workbench is used, then it is likely that the results of the SSADM analysis will be stored within a data dictionary, analyst workbench or CASE tool. The vendor may then supply tools that take analysis information from the dictionary or tool and automatically convert this into application outlines or even program code. The availability and sophistication of such tools is likely to have a significant impact on productivity.

In the assessment of such tools, the following points should be considered:

- the use of an integrated data dictionary to record the results of SSADM Analysis Phase activities and cross check them with AG design activities
- the use of an integrated, close or loose coupled analyst workbench to produce SSADM end

products

- the ability of the tools to produce SSADM requirements documentation for the maintenance phase of the life cycle

- the SSADM Support Tools Conformance Appraisal Scheme is now in place, which will test CASE tools' level of conformance to SSADM on a four point scale. The scheme is administered jointly by CCTA and the SSADM Research Centre (SRC) at Birmingham Polytechnic.

Are there tools available to map from analyst workbench or CASE tools into application code? Do such tools include links from the results of SSADM analysis?

Do such tools have any SSADM conformance scheme approval?

8 Quality and control

The rapid development of code and data structures requires that the AG provides good control and documentation of the resources (files, databases etc) used. This usually requires that the AG interfaces closely with the organisation's data dictionary and that the dictionary has sufficient access control and 'status' functionality.

8.1 Documentation

Documentation should be 'active' rather than 'passive'; ie the documentation should result from building a specification, not be a separate activity. Only in this way is consistency between documentation and application assured.

Can documentation of the application be generated as a by product of building the application?

8.2 Development control

The application generator, or its supporting dictionary, should allow multiple versions of the application components to exist concurrently; typically development, production and historic versions. This facility exists in those products supported by a good data dictionary, but few others. Otherwise, projects need to maintain separate production and development libraries themselves.

Separate libraries are essential in a realistic environment. Individual projects, users and production systems must be protected from each other. Note that some systems have a single central library that this effectively partitioned. A single library is likely to grow very large.

Does the generator allow the definition of separate development and production libraries?

On-line interactive development can be expensive in terms of computing resources. Frequently costing information relating to individual users/projects is required to provide a means of controlling access.

Does the application generator provide accounting information to enable the costing of application specification maintenance and development?

Version control and configuration management tools are increasingly in demand to control the development process.

Does the application generator provide mechanisms for managing 'versions' within 'releases' of the generated application?

8.3 Audit control

Because of the ease with which programs may be amended, it is essential that there is recognition of 'production status', where access to programs is strictly controlled. In addition, it may be desirable for audit and control purposes that the person seeking access be identified and the date and time be recorded.

It is likely to be an auditor's requirement that at least production libraries are protected against unauthorised access. Passwords are commonly used. Some systems rely upon facilities provided by the host operating system (for example separate files, each with the operating system's password access control mechanism applied).

How can the production libraries be protected from unauthorised use?

It may be an auditor's requirement to know when a program change has been effected. Ideally the system should write the date, time, user-id and program-id to a system log.

What information is logged when an application specification

- *has the source accessed?*

- *has the source amended?*

- *is recompiled into an application program?*

8.4 Quality assurance monitoring

Because of the more rapid development of applications, it is necessary for an organisation to monitor and control the quality of the code produced. The minimum requirements are the ability to

Chapter 8
Quality and control

determine what applications exist, what the interactions between routines and applications are, and who 'owns' them. Other requirements may be facilities to monitor and possibly prevent the use of particular constructs. Few AGs address this area.

Does the AG incorporate any facilities that can be used for Quality Assurance monitoring, for example utilities which scan or monitor applications and produce a statistical profile of where resources are used?

Can an application cross reference report be produced?

What controls are available to restrict use of particular AG facilities to specific users?

8.5 Performance monitoring and control

Some AGs contain very powerful file processing constructs. Used carefully they can be extremely effective; used wrongly, they can be very inefficient. The AG should contain facilities for gathering statistics on the use of such constructs and on the resources they consume. It is also desirable to be able to impose limits on the resources available to particular user authorisation levels to prevent inefficiency.

A major benefit of AGs, particularly when used with Relational DBMSs, is that they permit the end user to formulate his own ad hoc enquiries. Uncontrolled use of such a capability can, however, lead to serious performance problems.

Does the AG include accounting constructs to record the usage of the software and/or the resources used by the software?

Most DBMSs attempt to satisfy queries using some form of optimiser to perform the action in the most efficient manner. Some DBMSs will attempt to answer queries irrespective of the amount of resources used. What is required therefore is some form of governor that will estimate the amount of resource to be consumed by the transaction and will prevent the transaction being started or completed if this is deemed desirable.

Is there some form of governor?

Can the user/DBA change the conditions under which the governor operates?

How does this interact with the AG?

8.6 Effect on the organisation

The introduction of some products into a department is likely to have a much more significant impact on the way that department works than will other products. 'Tactical' products are those which can easily be introduced to solve immediate one off problems; they will involve a short educational and installation lead time. 'Strategic' products require a much greater commitment, in order to get the correct infrastructure into place, to use them effectively.

Strategic products also usually imply a commitment to using a true 'database' approach and to the use of a DBMS. Some products could be used for either.

Would you describe your AG as being for strategic or for tactical use?

What form of organisational infrastructure is recommended to make optimal use of the AG?

Does the product require a centralised data dictionary?

Does the AG documentation recommend the appointment of a Database Administrator (DBA)?

Is the AG part of an integrated set of products, for example DBMS, Data Dictionary, Office Automation etc?

Can the AG be used to develop and run completely separate applications or are all applications combined into a system at some level (perhaps due to the specification being held in a single library or possibly the run time code needs to run in a shared environment)?

Does the AG only interface to a fully functional DBMS?

9 Environment independence

Environment independence is important if it is likely that the application will be moved to another hardware or system software environment. An advantage of the AG approach is that the technical environment dependent aspects of the application are separated from the specification, which should allow the specification to be implemented on other environments with minimal changes.

This chapter refers to the environment in which the generator operates. This is not necessarily the same as that in which the generated application operates. The generator component consists of two parts: specifying the application and 'compiling' it. It is possible that these two could have different environments, but unlikely.

9.1 Hardware independence

To what extent is the AG tied to a specific hardware architecture. Does being tied to a hardware architecture tie the AG to hardware from a particular vendor.

Is the product specific to a particular hardware architecture?

Facilities available will be terminal dependent.

What type of terminals does the AG support (for example synchronous, asynchronous, character, bit mapped, colour etc)?

What user interface standards are supported?

9.2 Software independence

To what extent is the product specific to a particular operating system environment, is this environment that of the AG vendor. Does the vendor provide any commitment to conform to extant and forthcoming open systems' standards, for example OSI, X/Open, Posix, SQL.

Sometimes different variants of the product are available on different machines. In such cases, applications may not be portable. This may be reflected in some of the other answers.

If the application generator operates on a range of machines or under a range of operating and TP systems, at what level is portability achieved?

Generators which require batch facilities are usually less effective in a prototyping environment. Some vendors appear to try to hide the fact that a batch process is necessary as part of the generation process.

Do any components of the product require a batch environment? If so, which?

Application generation frequently makes full use of interactive development. It is useful to be able to do some of the application specification/generation in a batch mode if online terminals are scarce.

Can those components of the product which are normally used in an online environment also operate in a batch environment?

Required operating system modifications may cause support or maintenance problems.

Is it necessary to incorporate any non standard features within the operating system or the TP monitor to support the applications generator?

10 End user interface

The usability of the application is likely to be a major factor in determining the success of the implementation. While the look and feel of the application is largely dependent on the skills of the development team, they are constrained by the functionality of the product. The criteria below concern the environment that can be built for the end user. Note that some AGs operate in more than one environment, for example on bitmapped workstations as well as character based terminals.

It is normally true that providing a high quality user interface, perhaps using colour, or a bit mapped workstation, is likely to increase the cost of the project. It may often be the case, however, that the usability of the interface is what determines the ultimate success or failure of the project. Such factors should not be neglected, even at an early stage of a project.

10.1 Invocation

The user should be able to invoke the required application as easily as possible and with a minimum of keystrokes. The ideal is for the user logon with password to lead automatically into the application main menu.

Some systems do not differentiate between using the product to specify an application and using it to run an application. This is not the best approach when attempting to construct 'black box' application systems. Also, it is often advantageous to be able to merge the transaction processing system's logon procedure with the application's logon procedures to avoid the user having to sign on twice.

To use a generated on-line application, does the user

- *invoke the same logon sequence as used by the generator when specifying an application?*

- *invoke a logon sequence designed as part of the application?*

- *use the transaction processing monitor's standard logon sequence?*
- *other? (please specify).*

10.2 Navigation

Simple and consistent mechanisms should be available to enable the user to move from one field to another, or one screen to another.

What is the control mechanism to move from one screen (exchange) to the next?

- *the user specifies the transaction code of the next screen (exchange) explicitly*
- *the user is automatically returned to a central menu where he specifically selects the next exchange*
- *the application decides based upon the user's input*
- *the user chooses a course of action from a list of options (e.g. next screen, previous screen, exit etc).*

Function or control keys are used to switch states within an application and are therefore useful. However, their inclusion may depend upon the terminal's characteristics.

Are function keys supported? Are these programmer definable?

Can the developer change the keystrokes required for actions such as accept, abort etc, and the terminology used by the AG supplied form menus for example Add, Update, Query etc?

10.3 Dialogue

The application developer will design a dialogue for use by the end user. This dialogue will (normally and preferably) consist of a hierarchy of menus and forms. The capability of the workstation usable by the product, and affordable by the project, dictates the type of environment that can be built for the end user.

End users are becoming increasingly familiar with sophisticated interfaces and are beginning to demand the same functionality from an AG.

Are bitmapped workstations with mice supported?

Are pop-up or pull-down menus available?

What types of menu selection are available?

- *selection by mouse*
- *ring menu*
- *numeric designation*
- *alphabetic designation*
- *first character*
- *scroll and highlight using cursor keys*
- *other.*

Are windows supported?

10.4 Presentation and rendition

The appearance of what is seen on the screen is limited by the terminal or workstation. The application can be made much easier to use by careful design, including using the display rendition capabilities to differentiate between the different categories of information seen on the screen. The availability of graphics to permit lines, boxes, circles etc, to be drawn on the screen is also beneficial.

A range of different display capabilities will be required for general applications, but the selection may be constrained by terminal characteristics.

Can the following field attributes be specified within the AG?

- *protected*
- *hidden (not visible - used for passwords, etc)*
- *high brightness*
- *reverse video*
- *colour*

- *blinking*
- *font*
- *character size*
- *other (please specify).*

The availability of graphics enables the developer to build systems that can provide a familiar image to the user, for example by emulating existing manual forms.

Can the screen painter paint graphics, or at least graphics characters?

10.5 Variants

Often one dialogue can be made to suit the requirements of more than one user role. This would be where their requirements only differ slightly; perhaps some menu options are not available to one role, or perhaps the existence of certain fields are not disclosed.

One approach is to allow variant sets of forms to be retained with an indicator to link them to particular logons.

Can variants of the dialogue and forms be made available to different users or groups of users? How can this be achieved?

10.6 End user help system

Help systems reduce the training overhead and can be an essential learning aid for beginners, or occasional users of a facility. Help systems can either be full blown parallel applications, or can be simply pop-up windows which appear on request.

Can help screens be programmed?

Can the help system be generated automatically from the data dictionary?

Is help context sensitive?

Can the help system be browsed?

To what extent can the developer control how the user obtains help?

Is there a limit on help available at any level? If so what are the limits

10.7 Session concurrency

It is beneficial if the user can suspend one activity and invoke another, perhaps for cross reference purposes. This could be achieved by windowing, by multiple sessions, or by split screen working. Users are increasingly demanding this functionality - for example to answer telephone enquiries.

Can the user run more than one application at once? Can the second application be a dissimilar application, for example a word processor or mail system?

10.8 Error messages

Error messages should be clear, concise and meaningful; cryptic error messages do little to inspire user confidence.

Can the developer supply text to clarify the error messages emanating from the AG, the DBMS or from the operating system?

Is the error code supplied in this way actioned by

- *the operating system?*
- *the DBMS?*
- *being held and used by AG?*
- *the dictionary?*
- *other? (please specify).*

10.9 Skill levels

The requirements of experienced users are not the same as those of novice or occasional users. It may be beneficial to have 'short cut' or 'expert commands' for skilled users.

Does the system support the concept of different levels of user skill?

Can expert, 'short cut', commands be implemented?

11 Security

Security of the data, and of the application development tools that access it, is of vital importance to many projects. Use of the AG may bypass many of the underlying DBMS controls, hence control at the AG level is essential.

11.1 Access control

To what extent will the developed application allow different users to access only the functions to which they are entitled.

How can users be restricted to particular parts of the application, or from accessing particular datasets, tables or fields?

Does the AG rely on DBMS access controls?

Will the AG support access control devices such as badge readers etc?

Can users be restricted to particular tools or subsets of tools within the application development environment?

11.2 Encryption

It may be important, especially if using a distributed system, to be able to encrypt data within the AG.

Can the AG encrypt data or is it dependent on DBMS capabilities?

12 Product credibility

Application generators are frequently the subject of 'imaginative' marketing. Some AGs are produced by small or relatively unknown software houses or are written and supported in foreign countries and marketed here by agents. Other AGs are new to the marketplace and are therefore as yet untried. Such AGs are not necessarily of poor quality, but it is necessary to assess the likelihood of the software and the marketing agency still being viable in the future before committing to using the product, irrespective of its technical merit.

12.1 Quality of product

Application generators should be constructed to a high quality using rigorous, structured development and testing techniques.

Is the product specified using a formal definition language or method such as VDM or Z?

Does the product developer subscribe to and comply with the requirements of British Standard (BS) 5750 or equivalent documents? (This deals with a supplier's capabilities to operate a quality management system in the design, manufacture, installation, inspection and testing of a product).

Has the product been submitted to any independent authority (eg the National Computing Centre Ltd (NCC)) for evaluation or certification/validation? If so, are the results available? Are any independently reached performance figures available from such authorities?

What guarantees are there against defects in the product?

12.2 Product development status

Information on the development status of the product is essential before making a long term commitment to its use.

What is the current development stage of the product, for example:

- *static?*

- *stable but in the process of being cosmetically enhanced (ie minor changes and improvements in presentation, or the way(s) in which the product interacts with the user, are in preparation. Any such changes will not affect basic, user functions)*

- *being functionally enhanced?*

- *in the process of being developed for use on other machines?*

Have any enhancements been introduced recently? Are there any which are under development? If so please list planned enhancements and the target dates for the introduction of such enhancements.

When was the last major, new version (as defined by the supplier) released and when is the next major, new version planned for release.

How does the company determine when a system requires enhancement and the nature of the additional or supplementary facilities and features which are to be incorporated?

Are there any weaknesses which have been identified in the current version of the product?

What plans are there for the product over next 3 to 5 years? Will the product be different to today's version? If so, what differences will there be?

How is system updating arranged to take account of new developments and legislation?

Have any overseas products been Anglicized (eg date format, £ symbol)?

How many updates have been issued in the last year?

12.3 Supplier assessment

The supplier assessment will take into account the size of the supplier, whether they are the originators of the software or simply agents, how long they have been producing or marketing software, the size and whether they are a company based in Britain or abroad. The term supplier should be used in the widest sense ie where the supplier is not the developer, all organisations involved in the development, marketing and support of the AG should be investigated.

Some AGs are produced originally by small independent software houses and then marketed, sometimes under another name, by computer manufacturers. This section should help to identify such products. Also, products simply marketed rather than developed by a supplier are likely to enjoy a lower level of on-going support.

Name, address and telephone number of supplier.

Name(s), position(s), address(es) and telephone number(s) of the person(s) to contact for further details, if necessary, regarding

- Marketing information
- Technical support.

How long has the supplier been in operation

- in the UK?
- world-wide?

Was the product originally developed by the above supplier?

What organisations have used the supplier's services in the past?

Does the supplier have a range of products covering related topics, ie is it an area in which he specialises?

Is the supplier a subsidiary of any other company? If so, please give details.

How many years has the supplier been active in the development and/or marketing of application generators?

During the last year, what percentage of total revenue has been derived from application generators?

What percentage of total profit or income has been contributed to research and development of AGs? (ie future facilities, CASE, etc)

How many employees are dedicated to the development of application generators?

12.4 Product background

Most application generators start their life in a slightly unstable state; some never achieve stability. If an AG has a reasonable number of production field sites (not simply copies out for approval or copies distributed but not seriously used), then the product's capabilities and potential may be assumed to be at least adequate and the risk involved in selecting such a product is less than that of a new and untried package. New releases of a product may however be potentially risky.

Development ancestry

Potential buyers should establish when the 'product' was first available rather than the concept. Some application generators are developments of tools used internally by the supplier. Sometimes these early internal versions are quoted to imply that the product has a better 'history' than is the case.

When was the AG first installed at a customer site for customer usage?

What is the source and history of product(s) under consideration?

For how long has the AG been commercially available?

What was the development environment (ie the machine on which the AG was developed in the supplier's organisation)?

Did the supplier write the AG, or is he acting as agent?

Where is the software originator based, eg local, UK, Europe, America?

Development profile

Many AGs are still in a state of development and enhancement. New features, facilities and environments are being added. While this may provide many useful new features it may cause problems if releases with desirable new features appear during a development.

Note. New versions of application generators usually incorporate either significant improvements in functionality or in performance. New versions are typically released on an 18 to 24 month cycle. Intermediate releases tend towards fixing bugs only.

Chapter 12
Product credibility

How often are major product versions released? When was the last one released and when is the next one planned?

What enhancements, if any, are planned for the AG and when will they be introduced?

What is supplier policy towards compatibility between versions?

How does the AG supplier determine when a system requires enhancement and the nature of the additional/supplementary facilities which are to be incorporated?

Product usage

An indication of the numbers of users of the AG, the sales profile of the AG and other pieces of information such as product appraisal and evaluation reports can give a valuable insight.

How many user sites of the AG are there

- *in the UK?*

- *within Government?*

- *outside Government?*

- *elsewhere in Europe?*

- *elsewhere?*

How many systems of this type have been sold in the UK (and worldwide) during the past 12 months?

How many existing users are there (particularly any within government) and what is their volume of transactions (ie the number of applications currently in existence and use)?

For how long have earlier, or original, users stayed with the AG; or are all users (comparatively) recent?

Which is nearest competing product available in the marketplace?

Describe any previous projects using this AG with which the supplier has been involved both inside and outside of government. Please indicate the size and complexity of the jobs in broad terms.

Please give the name and address of reference site(s) which may be contacted if necessary.

Can other users be contacted, ideally in the same business area?

When was the first system of the type being considered (or proposed) successfully installed at a customer's site? Please provide details of the site's location and others, if available.

Does a user group exist for the product in question? If so, please state:

- *whether it was formed independently of the supplier's organisation*
- *how long such a group has been in operation*
- *how active is it*
- *the number of active members*
- *joining/ membership fees*
- *the number of meetings held each year*
- *when and where meetings are held?*
- *the name, address and telephone number of the group's secretary.*

How closely does the supplier collaborate with any such user groups which might be established?

Product information	Other sources of information other than those suggested by the product supplier can be valuable.
	Are there any independent reports and evaluations on the AG(s) being considered? Can copies of any reports be made available (IF NOT, WHY NOT?)?
User Profile	While many AGs are usable by a wide class of users, most products are best suited to particular user profiles. Best results will always be attained when the correct tools have been chosen for the particular user profile. Most suppliers will claim usability by all classes of user.
	Who are expected to be the principal users of the AG?
	• *non IT staff*

- *analysts*
- *novice programmers*
- *experienced programmers*
- *others (please specify)*.

12.5 Documentation

Application generators require adequate documentation. Frequently AGs at the beginning of their life, or AGs marketed by small organisations, appear with inadequate documentation. Other AGs appear with large amounts of poorly structured documentation.

What information is available about the AG before purchase?

What documentation is available, and how well is it presented?

What manuals and other documentation are provided when the AG is purchased?

What other 'optional' manuals are available?

Can the documentation be copied by the user for his own use only?

What is the target audience for each manual eg management overview, system designer, application programmer, operator, etc?

Are the manuals available online?

What information is available on the technical content of the system, eg:

- *record formats*
- *database structure*
- *parameter tables*
- *validation mechanisms*
- *source code?*

In the event of the supplier going out of business, what arrangements are there for access to the source code, eg is a copy of the source code lodged with an Escrow Agent?

Do customers use the documentation provided or is there a need to develop instructions which are specific to each installation?

12.6 Training

Application generator packages in particular usually claim to require relatively small amounts of training, but this is not always the case. Poor quality training will predispose staff against good products and may therefore affect a project's overall success. Note that length of training required is not a sufficient guide as this will depend on the complexity of the product.

Note that AGs suitable for end user use may require separate introductory courses for programmers and non programmers.

Please state whether training is included in the purchase price of the proposed software system and:

- *where such training is normally carried out*
- *whether onsite courses can be arranged*
- *the nature and amount of training normally required to operate and use the AG (based on the supplier's previous experience)*
- *the duration of training courses*
- *the individuals at which such training is aimed.*

Are appropriate training courses provided by the supplier?

Do any third parties offer training in the use of the AG?

How much computing expertise is required by attendees?

Please describe any additional training related to the efficient and effective use of the system including details of cost, location, duration and frequency.

12.7 Support

Support will be required, especially when an AG is first introduced and before the organisation has built up its own inhouse expertise. The type and level of

Chapter 12
Product credibility

support available will depend on the size of the supplier organisation and the number of sites they are supporting. There have been a number of instances where AGs have enjoyed rapid market success but this has resulted in their support services being thinly stretched or staffed by poorly qualified personnel. Support quality is also likely to be dependent upon where software development is done. If all development is done overseas, then the local knowledge of the internals of the software is likely to be reduced and the time taken to fix bugs increased.

Some AGs are purchased or marketed by UK suppliers, but not written by them. Where this is the case the level of UK support may be found wanting for newly established AGs.

General

Where and by whom is support undertaken?

Where are the support services located?

What is the policy for supporting previous releases of the AG and how many versions are currently supported?

To what extent is modification by users allowed without affecting support?

How are queries and problems dealt with after installation?

For which aspects of the implementation will the supplier be responsible (eg hardware and software installation, system and data conversion, user training)?

Pre-sales

Is a demonstration available?

What are the arrangements for a trial of the AG?

Does the right exist to reject the product if it fails user specified acceptance tests?

Will any verbal claims and promises made by sales people be written into the standard contract?

Who will provide support/answer queries, and how accessible are they, eg by telephone, office hours only?

Installation	*What maintenance and support services are available during installation of the AG?*
	Will specific personnel be allocated to this project (full or part time; at the beginning of, during and after implementation)?
Type and level	*What maintenance and support services are available once the AG is operational?*
	How many technical support staff are supporting how many users?
	How many technical support staff are available in the UK?
	Does the supplier operate a 'hot-line' service for urgent user enquiries and fault reporting? If so, is the service part of a system maintenance agreement and please state:
	• *the average response time*
	• *the longest response time*
	• *the way in which the system operates.*
	How long does it take for a supplier's hot-line to answer, and how long to resolve queries?
	Is there a charge for hot-line support?
	What procedures are available for reporting problems and what action and priorities are assigned to rectifying faults?
	Describe the circumstances in which onsite maintenance/ assistance would be given. Would such services be provided by a sales representative or by a software expert/engineer? What would be the contractual response time for a call for assistance?
Fault correction	*Are details of system faults and required corrections circulated regularly to users? Is the software supplied with all corrections applied or are the corrections (fixes) supplied separately for incorporation by the user?*
	How are faults corrected (for example, by means of a new software issue, letter of notification, onsite assistance; or by telephone contact)?

Are new versions of the AG automatically sent to users?

What are the escalation procedures for fault correction? When will the Managing Director become aware of a serious fault?

12.8 Enhancements

The methods and procedures by which enhancements to software products are handled are extremely important in the context of reducing or avoiding disruption during the introduction of enhancements or improvements to the package.

What arrangements can be made for future changes which may be required by the user?

What are the arrangements for future changes in requirements, and how will the work be costed?

How upward compatible is the AG for changes to

- *the hardware?*
- *the operating system?*

Are there facilities for users to 'customise' the AG?

12.9 Related products

Some AGs have 'core' or 'shell' application systems available; these could save development time (see the Application Software Packages volume).

Does the AG supplier market application products eg

- *personnel system?*
- *financial systems (eg general ledger)?*
- *others? (please specify)*

How are these products supported?

13 Project specific requirements

Any other requirements specific to the Departmental IT Strategy and/or project but not fully covered in other parts of this volume.

14 Costs

It is usually a strategic objective to minimise costs but this is subject to meeting other requirements. Often costs are tangible but benefits are intangible. Within the CCTA User Guides it is recommended that costs should be calculated over the life of a study or project usually between 5 and 10 years. While cost comparison is done in detail for the final selection of a product from the short list of approved products, there is also a case for including costing in the higher level formulation of that short list. For this purpose (ie software comparison), costing need not be done at a detailed or absolute level; approximate relative costs are sufficient.

14.1 Software

Software costs include a basic license cost plus usually a recurrent annual maintenance charge. When prices are given it should be indicated whether these are inclusive or exclusive of VAT.

What is the basis of sale (ie lease, rental, purchase) and is the software the subject of copyright? Please provide details of licence fees which may be appropriate and the way(s) in which the licence operates, eg site licence, single system, total organisation? If a licence only covers the use of a package on a single, identified computer system, can it be run elsewhere in an emergency?

How much does it cost to buy the product outright? Does this cost include a copy of the source code?

Can the product be acquired on a trial basis and if so for how long and what are the costs involved? Are these costs discounted from any subsequent purchase price?

Does the product require any particular separately purchasable prerequisites or components (software or otherwise) (from any vendor source)?

How much does it cost to rent or lease the product

- *per month?*
- *per year?*

What are the minimum and maximum rental periods?

What are your terms for multiple copies of the product

- on a single site?

- on multiple sites?

For the following customer support services, please give details of those which are available and the associated costs that are not included in the basic software charge:

- *design and configuration planning*

- *preliminary planning support*

- *development of clerical and operational procedures*

- *data and system conversion*

- *implementation.*

If customisation of the package is available from the supplier, what is the basis for charges, and how many staff are available for such changes?

What happens if we buy your system but, after several months cannot achieve the productivity gains claimed? Has this happened to other purchasers?

What installation support is included within the purchase price? Does the price include the cost of new versions?

Is any warranty provided?

Is software support provided? If so what is the cost?

14.2 Hardware

Hardware costs vary with different product sets. The existence of a TP monitor and of multi-threading software can reduce significantly CPU costs. If the product is to be installed on existing hardware, then enhancement of this hardware may be necessary.

As with software, hardware is likely to have an initial capital cost together with a recurrent maintenance cost. Costs may have to be considered for the system as a whole and not just the package element.

What is the cost of enhancement of existing hardware (for example additional disc and/or memory) in order to support the product?

Chapter 14
Costs

14.3 System operation and maintenance

System associated costs vary with the type of development tools used. 4GL tools will reduce development time and probably maintenance costs but will consume more hardware resources during development and operation. 3GL tools may produce efficient systems but take a long time to develop and may be more expensive and difficult to maintain. Different costs may be incurred depending on the type of licence, for example development or runtime. If purchasing the latter ensure that it includes all necessary facilities.

With certain types of product significant savings may be made by not purchasing unnecessary copies of development software (generators, editors, compilers, etc) in an environment where applications are run on multiple sites, but development is done centrally.

Please specify the scope and terms of the maintenance contract; and describe those services which are standard and those which are optional.

What are the maintenance/support costs and arrangements for corrections, upgrades and new releases?

Does the maintenance charge cover the issue of new software releases/ versions?

14.4 People

People costs are affected by factors such as the number needed, training requirements and their commercial worth. Sophisticated development tools reduce the number of people required for application development and probably reduces their training costs. However, such trained people may be commercially attractive and require a high salary to retain them. Sophisticated tools may require skilled infrastructure support and such people are likely to be expensive. Take on of new technology may require outside consultancy support that, while usually cost effective, will be expensive.

What is the cost of any training not provided free of charge when the product is purchased?

Please state whether training is included in the purchase price of the proposed software system and:

- *where such training is normally carried out*
- *whether on-site courses can be arranged*
- *the nature and amount of training normally required (based on your company's previous experience)*
- *the duration of training courses*
- *the individuals at which such training is aimed.*

Please describe any additional training related to the efficient and effective use of the system including details of cost; location; duration and frequency.

Is consultancy support available from the vendor? If so, what is the cost?

14.5 Documentation

Normally a package should be supplied with all relevant documentation necessary to operate it in an efficient and effective manner. Sadly some product's supplied documentation does not totally fulfil these requirements and additional documentation may need to be acquired. Some suppliers as part of their commercial pricing policy may choose to charge separately for appropriate documentation

What is the cost of any manuals not provided free of charge when the product is purchased?

Can manuals, once purchased, be copied for use only by the purchaser?

Criteria hierarchy

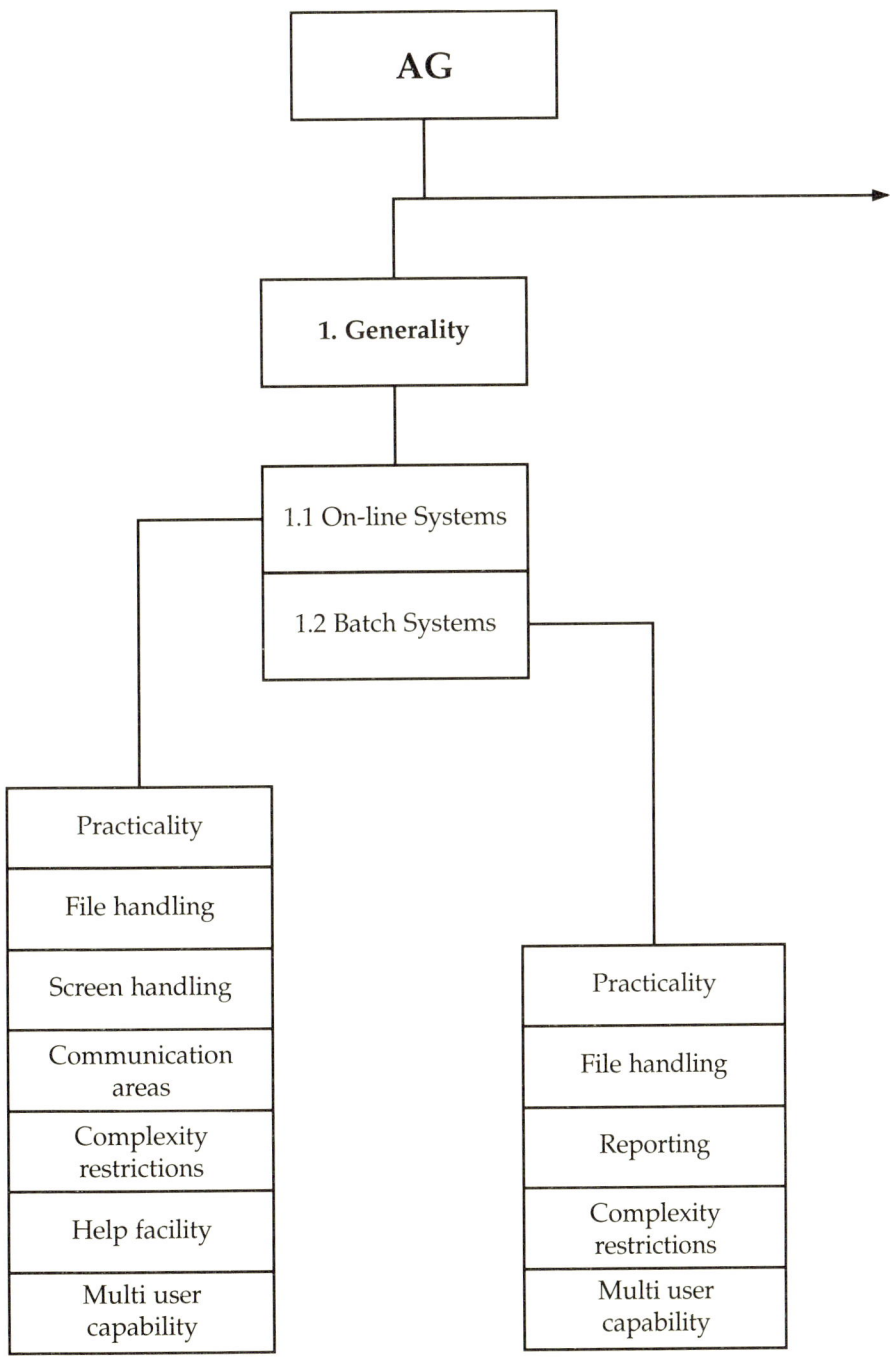

ISE Appraisal and Evaluation
Application Generators Volume

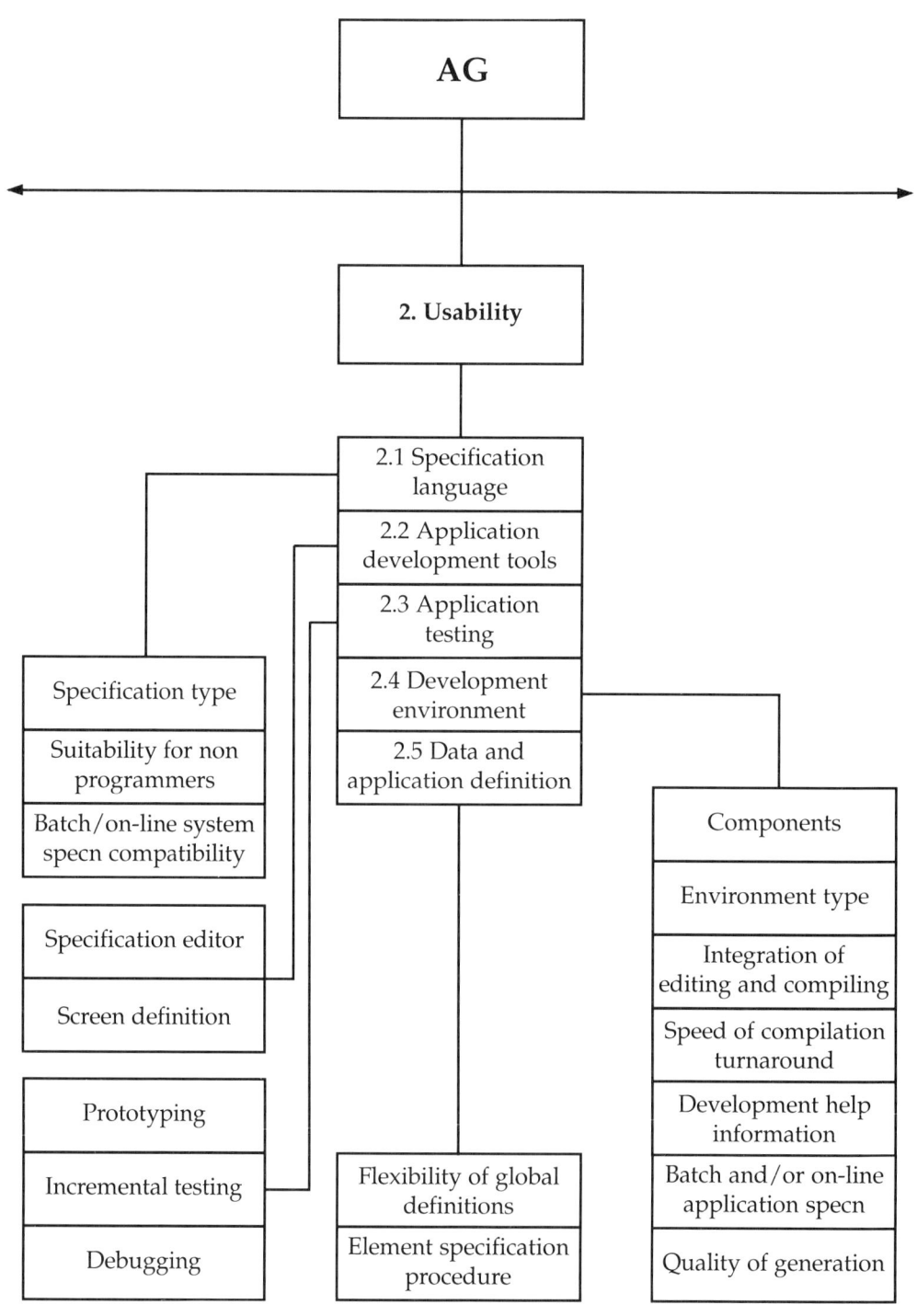

106

Annex
Criteria hierarchy

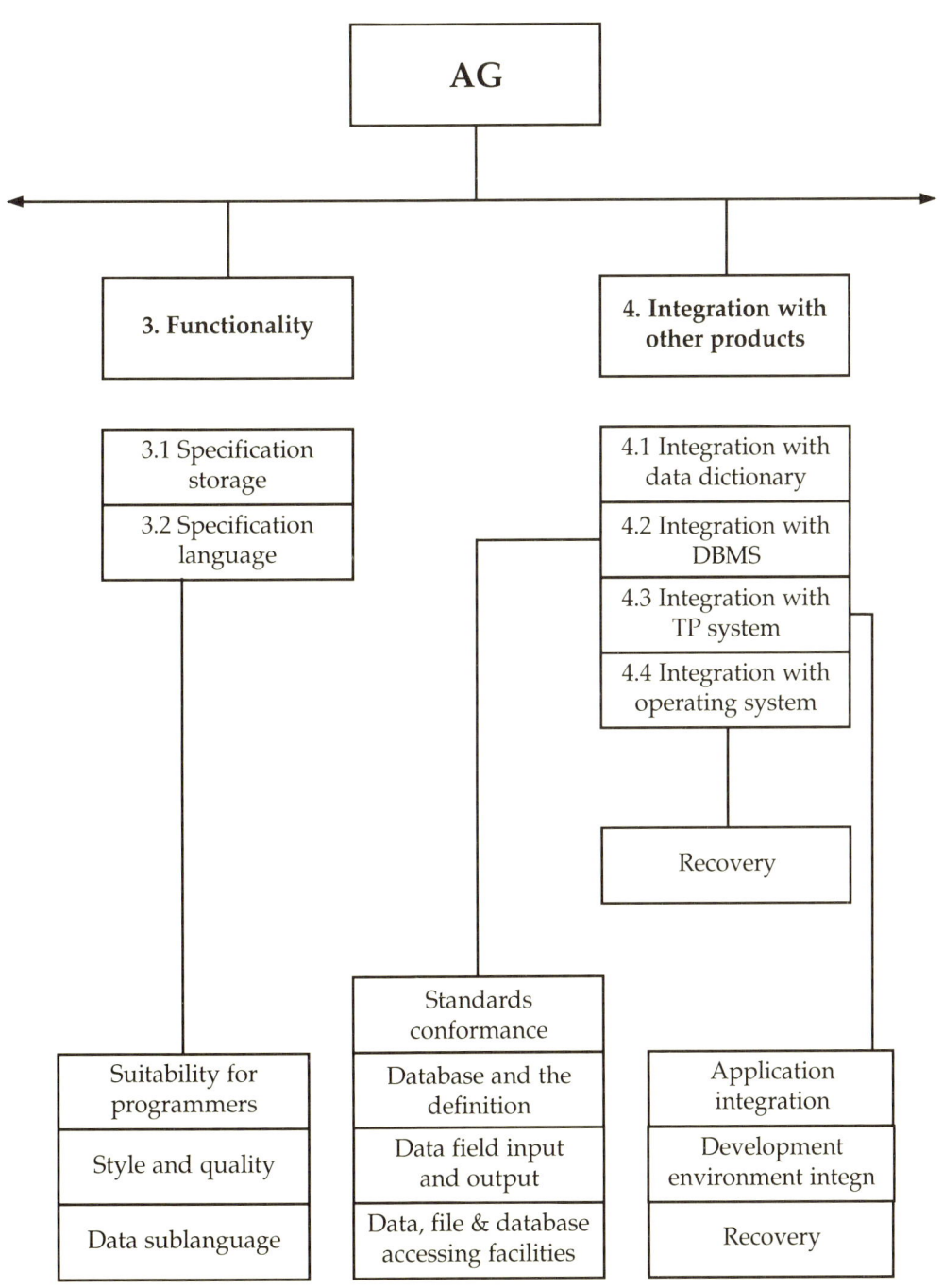

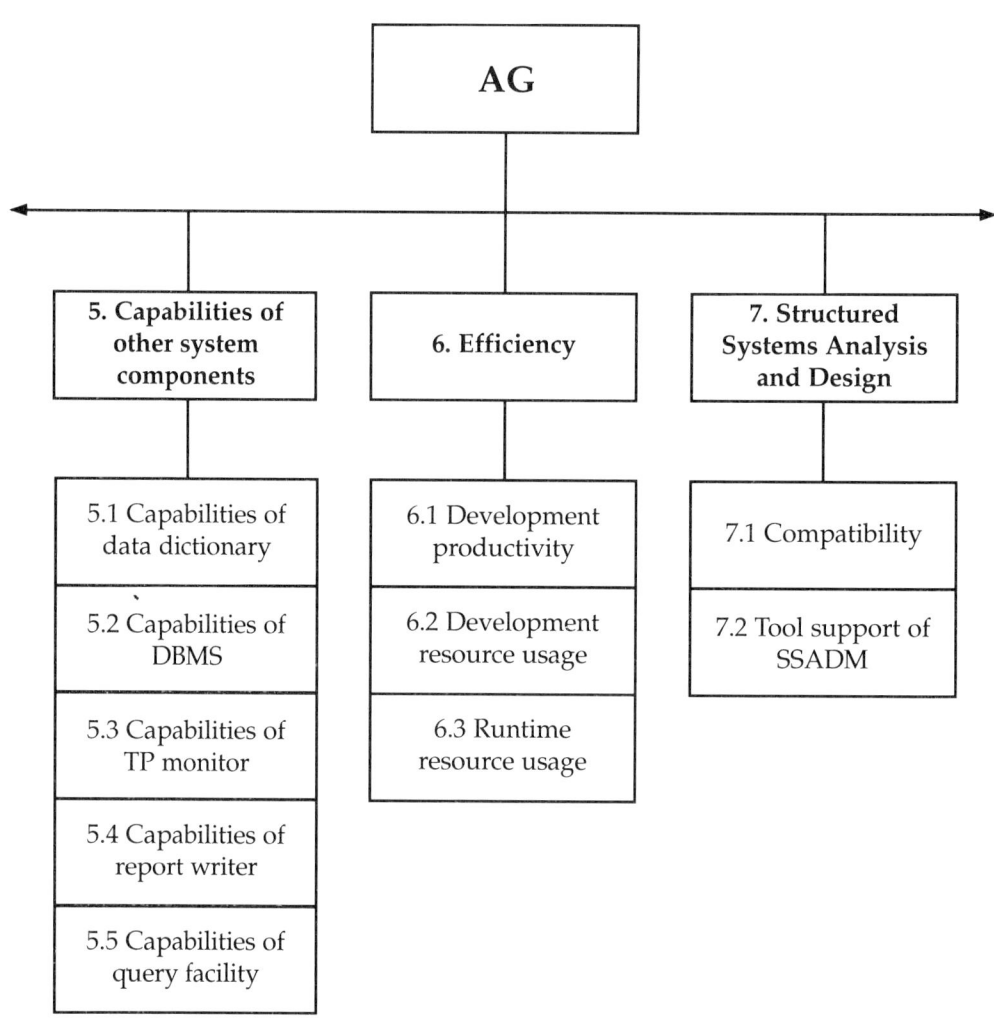

Annex
Criteria hierarchy

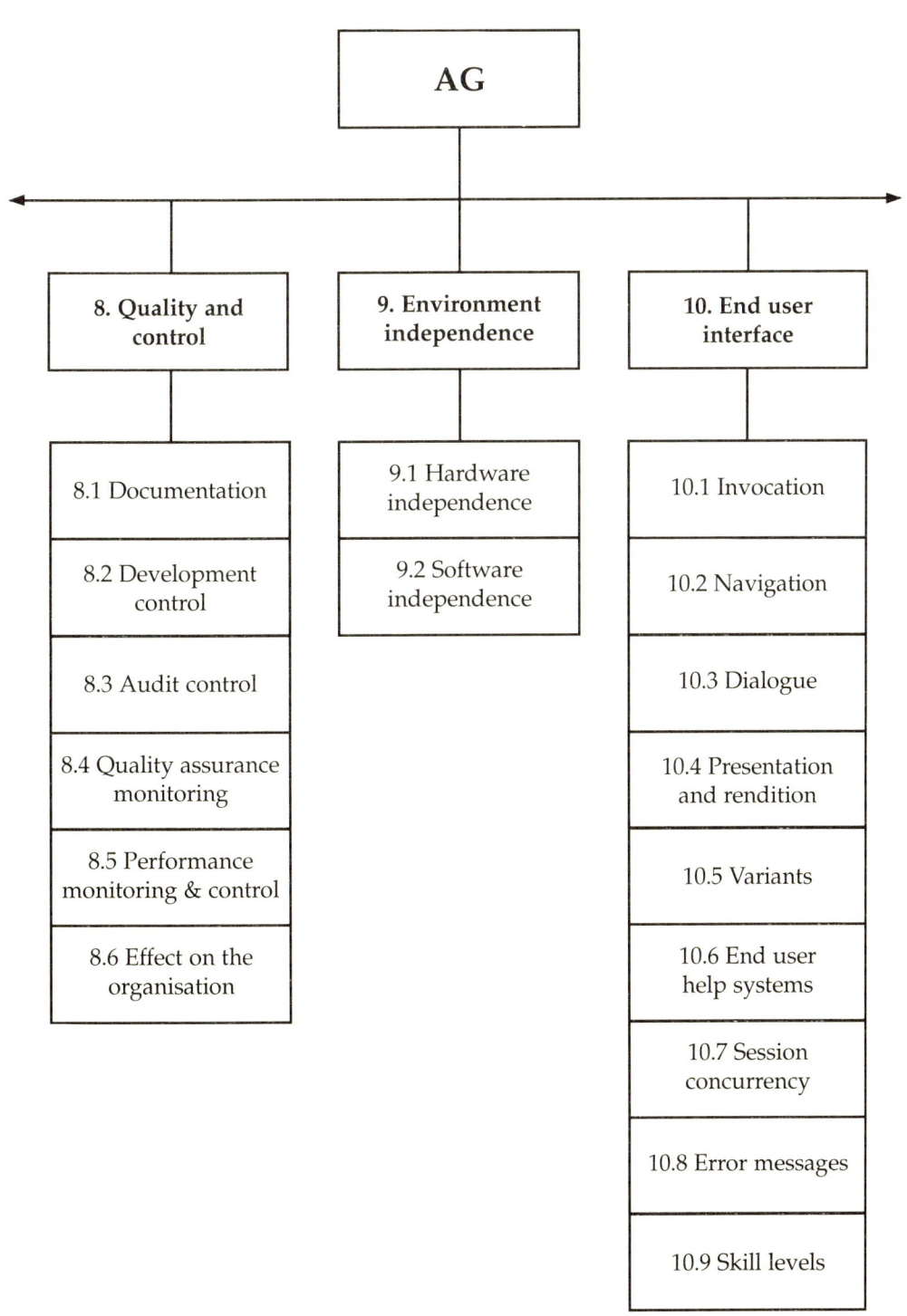

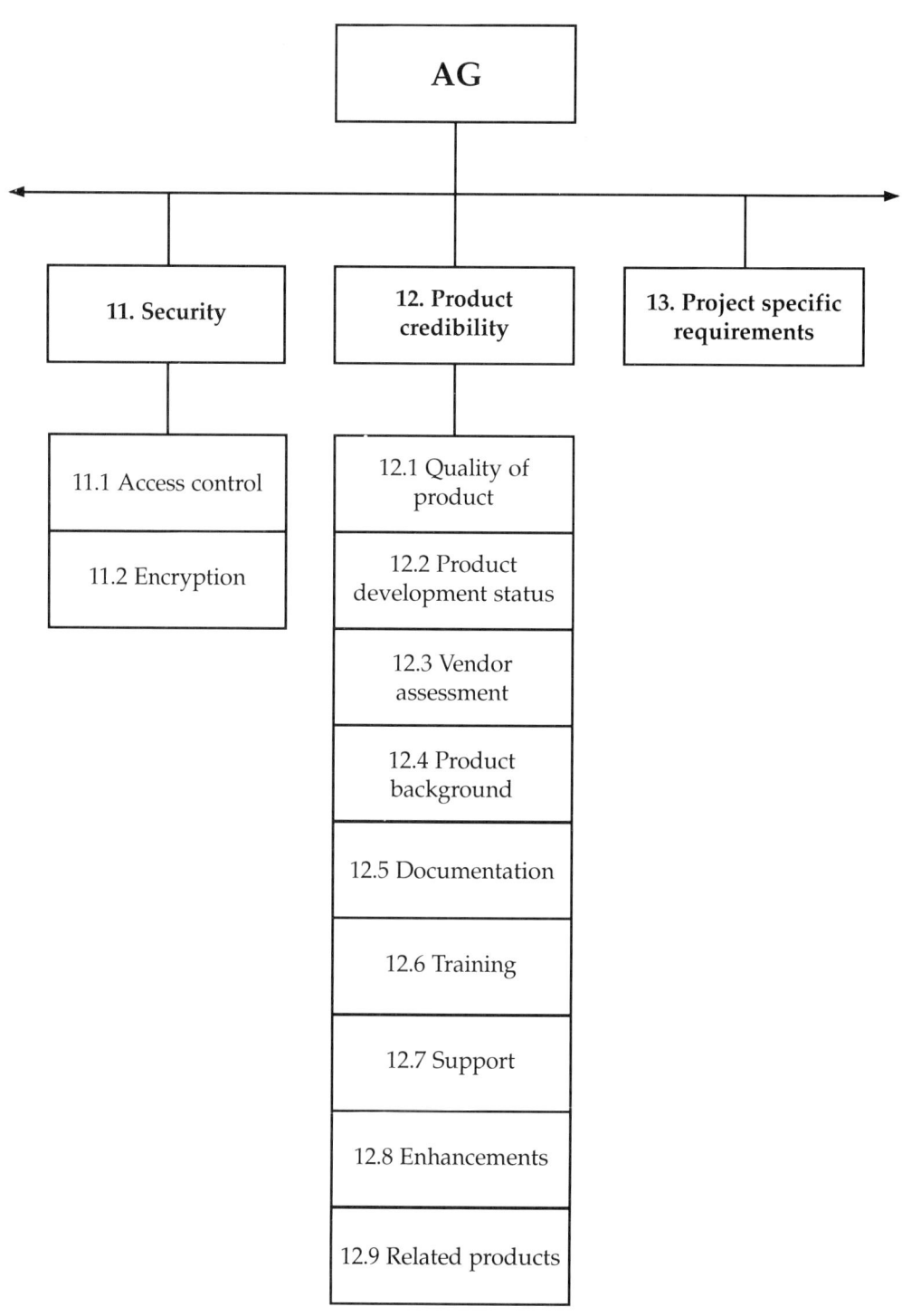

Annex
Criteria hierarchy

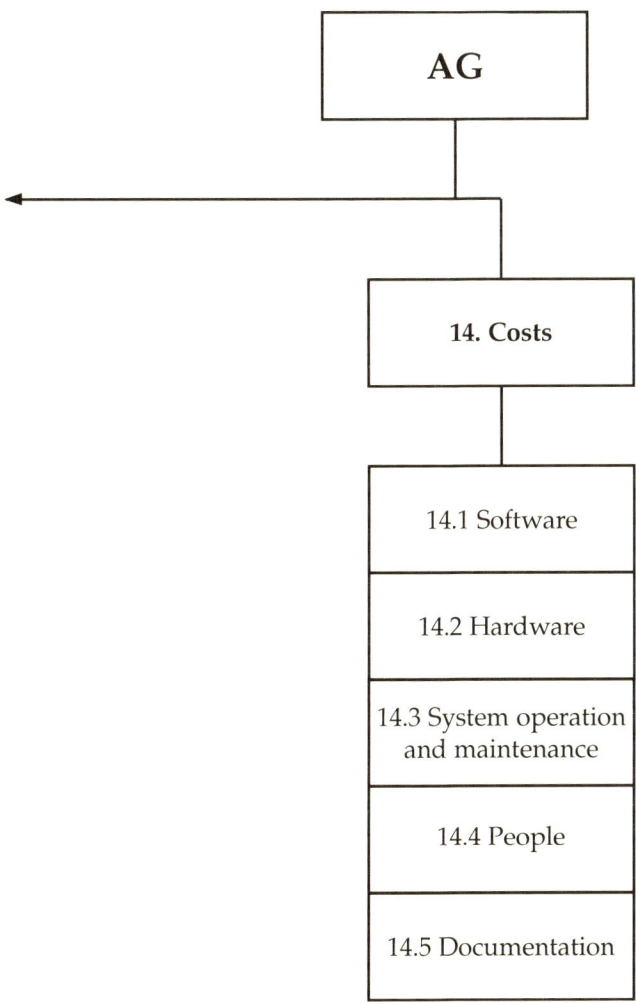

111